Organization Made Easy!

Tools for Today's Teachers

Frank Buck, Ed.D.

D1451928

EYE ON EDUCATION
6 DEPOT WAY WEST, SUITE 106
LARCHMONT, NY 10538
(914) 833–0551
(914) 833–0761 fax
www.eyeoneducation.com

Library of Congress Cataloging-in-Publication Data

Buck, Frank, 1959-
  Organization made easy! : tools for today's teachers / Frank Buck.
    p. cm.
  Includes bibliographical references.
  ISBN 978-1-59667-144-7
  1. School management and organization. 2. Orderliness. 3. Teachers—
Time management. I. Title.
  LB2805.B86 2010
  371.1—dc22

                                                    2009045852

10 9 8 7 6 5 4 3 2 1

Also Available from EYE ON EDUCATION

Get Organized!
Time Management for School Leaders
Frank Buck

Rigor is NOT a Four-Letter Word
Barbara R. Blackburn

101 "Answers" for New Teachers and Their Mentors:
Effective Teaching Tips for Daily Classroom Use
Annette L. Breaux

50 Ways to Improve Student Behavior:
Simple Solutions to Complex Challenges
Annette Breaux and Todd Whitaker

Classroom Motivation from A to Z
Barbara R. Blackburn

Classroom Instruction from A to Z
Barbara R. Blackburn

Seven Simple Secrets:
What the BEST Teachers Know and Do!
Annette Breaux and Todd Whitaker

What Great Teachers Do *Differently*:
14 Things That Matter Most
Todd Whitaker

How the Best Teachers Avoid the
20 Most Common Teaching Mistakes
Elizabeth Breaux

Leading School Change:
Nine Strategies to Bring Everybody on Board
Todd Whitaker

Great Quotes for Great Educators
Todd Whitaker and Dale Lumpa

Engaging Teens in Their Own Learning:
8 Keys to Student Success
Paul J. Vermette

Dedication

This book is dedicated to my wife and best friend, Davonia.
She is my inspiration. Her love and encouragement over our
more than 20 years of marriage made possible this book and
so many other joys in my life.

Acknowledgements

The thoughts in this book have been shaped by a lifetime of experiences and by interactions with very special people. While their mentions hear are brief, their contributions have been significant and lasting. I would like to express my appreciation:

- ◆ To Bob Sickles and the staff at Eye On Education for their confidence in me and their ever-present assistance.

- ◆ To Harry Anderson, the best first principal a teacher could ever have.

- ◆ To Dr. Henry Clark, my mentor in school administration. He showed me the difference one person could make in a school.

- ◆ To Pattie Thomas, my friend and the best coworker of my career. Her enthusiasm for learning something new every day is contagious.

- ◆ To Dr. Joanne Horton, my superintendent. She constantly nurtures potential in those around her.

Special thanks to those who contributed their ideas to this book:

- ◆ Jen Brown, French and Spanish teacher in Draper, Utah.

- ◆ Jenny Cheifetz, owner of the Sugar Mommy, LLC in New Hampshire (www.The SugarMommy.com) and former elementary school teacher.

- ◆ Ray Cheshire, high school science teacher at Bradford Academy in West Yorkshire, England.

- ◆ Sandra Hutchinson, first grade teacher at Seaside Elementary School in Torrence, California.

- ◆ Kerry Palmer, middle school principal at Trinity Presbyterian School in Montgomery, Alabama.

- ◆ Pattie Thomas, principal at Raymond L. Young Elementary School in Talladega, Alabama.

About the Author

Frank Buck served as a central office administrator, principal, assistant principal, and band director during a career in education spanning almost 30 years. He has served as an editorial advisor for the National Association of Elementary School Principals and has authored articles published nationally aimed at helping others become better organized and better managers of their time. The workshops he has conducted over more than a decade have drawn rave reviews from teachers and school administrators alike.

Dr. Buck resides in Pell City, Alabama, and serves as a consultant to schools and businesses. He can be contacted for workshops or speaking engagements through his website www.FrankBuck.org.

Contents

1

The Universal Challenges of Time Management and Organization

In *The Harried Leisure Class* (1970), Staffan Linder begins with the following poem:

> *Good-by, Sir, excuse me, I haven't time.*
> *I'll come back, I can't wait, I haven't time.*
> *I must end this letter—I haven't time.*
> *I'd love to help you, but I haven't time.*
> *I can't accept, having no time.*
> *I can't think, I can't read, I'm swamped, I haven't time.*
> *I'd like to pray, but I haven't time.*
>
> — Michel Quoist

The time constraints, and feelings which accompany them, are typical of our culture. In the forty years that have passed since that book's publication, the pace of society has grown more frantic. The demands of a changing world translate into increased demands on our time, and it seems to get worse with each passing year. Technology, with its promise of making our lives easier, has provided us with cell phones which ring constantly, a daily barrage of e-mails, and a general overload of information. The "time crunch" causes stress, and teachers are hungry to find relief from the stress and want to feel in control of their days.

It is possible not only to survive, but to thrive, in an age of limited time and unlimited demands. This book shows how. Teachers will find specific tools aimed at organizing surroundings, managing time, and increasing productivity.

Many published books address personal organization and time management. The topics are also favorite subjects of magazine articles. This popularity illustrates both the importance of these topics to our culture as well as how elusive mastering them can be.

My first book, *Get Organized! Time Management for School Leaders*, was written to fill a void in the literature. Too often, time-management books target the business executive. Although it is true that those in the educational arena share many of the same challenges, it is also true that schools are unique places. I provided a book that recognized that uniqueness. Since its publication, the book has found a particular niche with school administrators. Feedback has described it as being "practical" and an "easy read." Mission accomplished!

This book is written for *teachers*. In particular, my focus is on three groups of teachers. In the first group is the beginning teacher who overnight inherits a classroom which may well have been left in disarray by the predecessor. Without a system for organizing the surroundings and cataloguing the newly acquired responsibilities, the excitement of landing the job can quickly give way to a feeling of being overwhelmed by it. Colleges of education rarely prepare their students for the volume of responsibilities which will come their way.

In the second group is the experienced teacher who is new to that particular school. Regardless of how well organized and familiar one's old classroom was, walking into the new classroom brings back the feeling of being a new teacher. Every school has its unique rituals, routines, and procedures, and the learning curve can be steep. The teacher needs a system that will transform a room left in chaos. The teacher also needs a system that will take responsibility for organizing and remembering everything that must be done in those early days and weeks.

In the final group is the teacher who has come to the conclusion that it is time to "turn over a new leaf," and has the suspicion that life does not have to be as hard as he or she is making it. This teacher is the one who we hear saying, "I've got to get organized!"

Time-management books tend to offer a smorgasbord of suggestions, yet fail to provide the necessary depth to make a difference for the reader. This book provides the teacher with a complete system for managing time, getting organized, and staying organized.

Finally, the role of technology in our lives has increased exponentially in a relatively few years. The hallmark books on time-management and organization from decades past are unable to help us in this area. Publications such as this one are needed to address both the problems technology poses and the opportunities to harness the capabilities technology can offer.

This book will not eliminate the time demands that go hand-in-hand with this profession. What it can do is provide some tools and techniques to help the busy teacher address those demands more efficiently and effectively. The results will be a feeling of being in control of the day, a decrease in stress, and an increase in the sheer joy that the profession can offer. Moreover, the teachers will find more time to spend on that which is truly significant—perhaps on some of the quests outlined in the poem which began this section.

The Universal Time Crunch

If you feel the crunch of too much to do and too little time in which to do it, welcome to a very large club. In the 1972 classic book *The Time Trap*, Alec Mackenzie states, "Of the thousands of managers I have polled, from board chairmen and chief executives to first-line supervisors, only one in a hundred has enough time." Peter Drucker's 1966 hallmark work, *The Effective Executive,* tells us that "Effective executives…do not start with their tasks. They start with their time." Drucker goes on to say, "Nothing else, perhaps, distinguishes effective executives as much as their tender loving care of time." What Mackenzie and Drucker found to be true in the business world then is just as true in the arena of education today.

Organization, Time Management, and the Art of Teaching

Teaching is a blend of art and science. It is a complex discipline where theories regarding best practice change rapidly. Great teachers constantly expand their knowledge bases. They continue to learn. They communicate with other teachers. They challenge their assumptions. They spend time learning to use technology. They view change as a friend. They realize what was true yesterday will not necessarily be true tomorrow. Few things are constant in education. There is one element, however, that is unchanging. That element is *time,* accompanied by the feeling that there is never enough of it.

Some may dismiss attention to organization and time management as being separate from teaching. Nothing could be farther from the truth. Every good thing we do for our students, our school systems, our communities, our families, and ourselves is accomplished through the dimension of time. Furthermore, time is finite. We cannot buy, beg, borrow, or steal any more. We can only manage the 168 hours we are given each week. Our ability to plan, to enlist the help of others, and to achieve our goals is directly related to our ability to organize our environments efficiently and use time effectively.

How This Book Will Help

The ability to organize and manage time is crucial to our professional success, yet it is neglected in our preparation for that profession. For more than a decade, I have led workshops in these areas. The feedback I have received from participants is that the tools shared with them truly do make a difference in their productivity. Every time I hear the comment, "You changed my life," I am more convinced than ever that these concepts are teachable, and with a little practice, become second nature.

In this book, I share those tools with you. After reading the book, you will have a comprehensive system for bringing order and control to your personal and professional life. What you will read is practical and easy to implement. Do not be surprised when your level of stress diminishes as your level of organization and time management increases. Your focus can be on the present and on the joy in the moment.

2

Handling the Paper Blizzard and Decluttering Your Room

A place for everything, everything in its place.
— Benjamin Franklin

The teacher's desk can easily resemble a mountain of paper. That mountain can easily spread to window sills, surrounding tables, and every available flat surface. Work to be graded, graded work to be returned, notes from parents, material from committee work, and assorted books make finding *anything* tough. In addition, the new teacher inherits a classroom that may have been left in disarray by the predecessor.

How great it would be if the papers that sit on our desks would go away and magically come back exactly when we need them! That is exactly what this first tool will do.

I first saw this concept as a young boy during visits to my dad's office. He was a lawyer operating in a one-man shop. With no secretary, bookkeeper, or associate, he handled every aspect of his practice by himself. I noticed the first thing my dad did each morning was to open one filing cabinet drawer. In that drawer were files labeled with numbers from 1 through 31. If the date was the fifteenth day of the month, he pulled out the "15" folder. In that folder were papers related to the various people he would be seeing that day. Every piece of paper he would be working with that day was contained in that folder.

I thought my dad originated this idea, and it was one I put into practice from my first day as a teacher and have never left it. Later, I learned that it is an old and very common tool in the business world called the "tickler file."

Setting Up a Tickler File

Creating a tickler file requires nothing more than forty-three folders and a convenient place to put them. The first thirty-one folders are labeled 1 to 31, with each file representing a day of the month. The remaining twelve folders are labeled January through December, representing the twelve months of the year. The system is ready to go.

The idea is simple. When paper arrives that will be needed sometimes in the future, decide when you would like to see the paper again and drop it into the appropriate file. If the paper is going to be needed within the next month, slip the paper into the correct numbered folder. A piece of paper dropped into folder "17" will resurface on the seventeenth day of the month. For papers which will be needed again more than a month in the future, drop the paper into the correct *monthly* folder. The paper not needed until sometime in November is filed in the "November" folder.

At the end of the month, the folder representing the next month is emptied into the 1–31 folders. For example, at the end of February, the "March" file is opened, and a decision is made about what *day* in March each item is needed. The papers are then filed in the 1–31 folders.

Tickler files must be kept close at hand so that papers can be dropped into them throughout the day. For this reason, select a file drawer in the desk. While manila folders may be used for the tickler files, hanging files offer several advantages:

1. They stand upright and will not slide down in the drawer.

2. Their sturdy construction makes them excellent for the steady use they will receive.

3. They slide back and forth easily on their rails.

4. Manila file folders containing papers related to a particular project can be placed inside them.

Many teacher desks are not equipped with rails for hanging files. Any office supply store will carry a hanging file system that can be assembled in minutes.

Tickler files, when used properly, will receive a great deal of use. For this reason, choose high-quality files. Stagger the position of the labels so that tabs are not hidden behind each other. Label the tabs neatly. Be sure the drawer is large enough to hold the set of files comfortably and that the drawer slides easily. A teacher's world moves quickly. Anything that makes the system the least bit cumbersome will cause that system to sit idle in no time.

Tickler Files in Action

Let's begin with an example that is all too common. Imagine receiving the memo outlined in Figure 2.1.

Figure 2.1. Memo to Teachers

> **Memo**
>
> **To:** Teachers
>
> **From:** Principal
>
> Please complete this form and bring it with you to the faculty meeting on Tuesday.

This job actually has two parts:

1. Complete the form.

2. Bring the form to the meeting.

Completing the form is something that could probably be done on the spot. In fact, if a task will take only a few minutes to complete, you should complete it when it first appears. If you are going to take the time to look at it, completing it right then will save having to refamiliarize yourself with it later.

The second part of the task is the part that causes the trouble. The form has been completed and today is only Wednesday. What are you going to do with this piece of paper from now until Tuesday of next week?

In all too many classrooms, the drill resembles the following scenario. The paper is carefully placed on the corner of the desk so as not to be forgotten. For the next half-day, that paper is moved around in an effort to find other papers under it and around it. You look up from the current work countless times and see that piece of paper, each time thinking about how you must remember to take it to the meeting next week. Just after lunch, a student places a piece of makeup work on top of it. You have just experienced the beginning of the end!

By Tuesday, this piece of paper is buried seven layers down and has not been given a thought in days. You leave for the faculty meeting, and guess what is still buried on your desk? You realize dropping papers on the corner of the desk doesn't work!

The next time, you try a different approach. "I'll tape it to the wall," you think. "That way it won't get lost." This time, as you leave for the faculty meeting, where is the form? More than likely, it is still taped to the wall. One of those little rules of life is that whatever is taped to a wall becomes part of the décor!

An easier way exists. In this case, the memo needs to resurface on Tuesday. Simply drop it in the tickler file that corresponds to Tuesday's date. It is out of sight and out of mind. Furthermore, it is not cluttering the desk or decorating the wall. On Tuesday morning, you pull the folder for that day and dump it on the desk. There is the form along with any other papers that at some time in the past you wanted to see again on this particular day.

Other Examples

What else might be placed in the tickler files? Here is a partial list of possibilities:

◆ Tickets arrive for an event that occurs three weeks from now. Drop them in the numbered file corresponding to the date of the event. On that date, the tickets appear. No need exists to add them to an already cluttered purse or wallet for fear of forgetting them on the concert date. Nor will they be slipped into a nearby drawer and forgotten. Instead, on the day they are needed, they appear.

◆ Birthday cards need to be bought for friends and relatives. Buy all of them with one trip to the card shop. After arriving at home, address all of the envelopes and attach return address labels to the whole batch. Pencil in the date each card needs to go in the mail, and do so in the spot where the postage stamp will later go. Simply drop the cards in the appropriate tickler folders. Throughout the year, cards will appear on the exact days they need to go in the mail. Sign the card, seal and stamp the envelope, and drop it in the mail. You will never forget a birthday again!

◆ A flyer arrives outlining the driving directions for an upcoming workshop. You will need that item on the day of the workshop, so put it in the tickler file. It will appear the morning of the workshop.

◆ While completing a report for one of the school committees of which you are a member, you see that you do not have all of the information needed. Rather than allow the report to sit on the desk, jot down in your "signature tool" what information you need to obtain and make a plan for how you will get it. The "signature tool" is defined and explained in the next two chapters. Slip the report into a tickler file for several days in the future. When the report resurfaces, complete it using the newly gained information.

- A "problem of the day" is one of the resources you use for your classes. Drop each one in the appropriate tickler file.

- The test for the current chapter is prepared and ready to duplicate, but the copier will be out of order until Thursday. Drop the test in the file for Thursday. It will be out of sight and out of mind until the day you can do something about it.

- Thursday arrives and the test is now duplicated even though you will not give it until Wednesday of next week. After all, that copier could go down again! Put the test copies in a manila folder and put the whole folder in next Wednesday's tickler.

- Makeup work is being submitted, and you wish to grade it all in one batch. Pick a day for this task. As makeup work rolls in, throw it in that folder.

- You wish to pay all of your bills in one sitting a couple of times per month. As they arrive, throw them in one tickler folder and pay them all at one time when that date arrives.

For the teacher who is new to the profession or new to the school, the ticklers files serve another very valuable function. In each job I have held, the early days involved going through papers left behind by the last person. Many of them begged the question, "What do I do with *this*?" The best answer in many of those cases was simply to put it in the tickler file and let it resurface a month later. With another month of experience in that job and in that location, I knew exactly what those miscellaneous papers meant the next time they appeared.

Daily Ritual

For the tickler file to work, checking it daily must become habit. This ritual can be either the last thing before leaving in the afternoon or the first thing in the morning. A good feeling does exist when all of tomorrow's paperwork has been sorted before the day begins, and the first thing to attack the following morning is left squarely in the middle of the desktop—the otherwise *clean* desktop.

In this example, the date will be September 27. Figure 2.2 illustrates how the tickler files will look.

Figure 2.2. Example of Tickler File

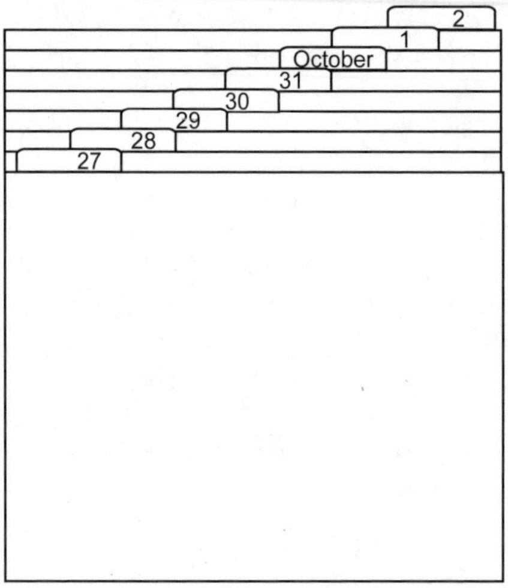

```
                                              ┌───2───┐
                                         ┌──1──┐
                          ┌─October─┐
                       ┌──31──┐
                 ┌──30──┐
            ┌──29──┐
      ┌──28──┐
  ┌──27──┐
```

As today is September 27, the "27" folder will be in the front of the drawer. The contents will be emptied on the desk. The proper place for the "27" folder is now in the back of all of the numbered folders, right behind folder "26." This file now represents *October* 27. Notice that the file for the next month, October, sits as a divider between those files representing days in September and those representing days in October. In addition, once October 1 arrives, the "October" folder will be in the very front, serving as a reminder to divide its contents among the 31 folders behind it.

On the desk will be all of the papers that at sometime in the past you had decided you should be seeing on September 27th such as the following examples:

- ♦ The birthday card that needs to go in the mail today.

- ♦ The tickets to tonight's concert.

- ♦ The driving directions for how to get to the concert.

- ♦ The folder of materials to discuss with Penelope's mom with whom you have a conference this afternoon.

- ♦ The phone message to call Mr. Jones. When you tried to call him last week, his secretary said he would be out of town until the 27th.

In this section, we have examined both personal and professional examples of using the tickler file. The tickler file is not just a tool for school.

Having an additional set of tickler files at home is a great idea. That way, no matter whether at home or school, papers you need in the future will be filed away where they are sure to return at exactly the right time.

Forgetting Is a Good Thing

Much of the stress in life is related to the many responsibilities teachers in today's world are expected to remember. From the examples presented in this chapter, it becomes obvious that tickler files relieve that stress by doing the remembering. When you drop a piece of paper in the tickler file, *you can now forget about it*. In fact, the entire system outlined in this book will require you to remember *exactly two things*. *One* of them is to check the tickler file first thing in the morning. The second is to look at the *signature tool*, either paper or digital, which will be examined in the upcoming two chapters.

"But what if I forget to check my tickler files?" exclaims an overwhelmed teacher. This question is typical of someone who half-heartedly uses the tool. Although some items are in the tickler file, this person also has papers all over the desktop. Busy working with this pile of papers, the thought of still more being in the tickler file never occurs.

Consider for a moment what the teacher who properly uses the tickler files will witness: a completely clean desktop. *Everything* is filed for the date it will be needed. Few people would face a clean desktop and not suspect there was paper to be handled somewhere!

One Little Memo Pad

For the first several years of my teaching career, my organizational system consisted of a memo pad in my shirt pocket and my tickler files. Any new ideas or commitments went straight onto the memo pad with one sheet being devoted to each item. Part of the daily routine was to drop each of those slips of paper into the tickler file. Each morning, the tickler file for the day would contain a variety of slips of paper for me to put in the order in which I wanted to accomplish them. I then had my marching orders for the day!

That system was enough to get me started. It may be enough to get the beginning teacher started. For the veteran teacher who lacks a system, the notepad may be enough to begin the road towards being a master of one's tasks instead of letting the details fall through the cracks. As one assumes larger and varied projects within the school, the tools needed for the job will change. The chapters on the "signature tool" will provide that support. When the number of tasks and projects is large and the ability to retrieve any piece of it instantly is desirable, the search capabilities of a *digital* signature tool will be necessary.

Three Little Boxes

Tickler files allow for a clean desktop. During the day, however, every teacher will deal with three types of paperwork and need places to put them:

- New paperwork just arriving.

- Papers from today's tickler file that cannot be completed immediately.

- Work produced that will now need to go to someone else.

Three boxes will organize the three types of paperwork:

In

In provides a place to throw anything new. The benefit is being able to continue focus on the task at hand without being distracted by every incoming piece of paper. During the typical day, a variety of items cross the desk:

- Today's mail.

- Memos from others in the school.

- Notes from parents.

- Phone messages.

Stop to examine and handle every piece of paper as it arrives, and the constant interruptions will prevent the accomplishment of much of anything. "In" provides a spot where all of the incoming barrage can be housed until it can be handled. "In" can take a number of physical forms. An inexpensive letter tray is an excellent choice. A file folder will work. An empty desk drawer is also a possibility.

Getting to the bottom of the Inbox must be *one single activity*. One goes to the mailbox at home and removes *all* of the mail, sorts it all, and handles it in one sitting. Likewise, the Inbox is a place where papers collect. Handling the entire stack must be a single task, not a day-long marathon. Many people complain of never being able to reach the bottom of the Inbox. The great fear is that somewhere towards the bottom lurks an emergency. The secret here is to make a decision on what each piece of paper represents:

- Throw junk mail immediately into the trash can. Throw away virtually all catalogs. Use the Internet to search vendor sites there rather than filing catalogs and purging them when new ones arrive.

- Tag items that can be handled by other people with an appropriate note to them and place in "Out."

- Return quick phone messages as soon as the paper is touched. Depending on the nature of call, handling other papers while carrying on the conversation is an option.

- Place reading material together in a folder or in one section of a briefcase. Before leaving for a meeting, grab some of it. While waiting for a meeting to start, waiting at a doctor's office, or waiting for a train to pass, having reading material at hand turns wasted time into productive time.

- Place items which will be handled on some future day in the appropriate tickler file.

- Some items will take time to complete. Make a quick decision on what needs to be done, add the item to the task list, and then place the paper into "Pending."

Pending

Some papers cannot be acted on immediately yet will be needed later in the day. *Pending* provides a holding tank for them. For example, today's tickler file includes papers related to a conference to be held with Penelope's mother this afternoon. *Pending* provides a place to put those papers until the time of the conference. *Pending* could be a letter tray. A desk drawer can just as easily be devoted to this function.

Out

This box houses the papers that need to go somewhere else other than the classroom (or office for nonclassroom teachers). These items would include:

- Outgoing mail.

- Material for someone else to file.

- Papers to go somewhere else in the building.

- Items to be taken home. If a briefcase is kept near desk, these items could be placed there.

At one or more times during the day, emptying *Out* will be one single activity. As with *In* and *Pending*, *Out* can be a letter tray, a desk drawer, a folder, or a neat stack placed under a decorative paperweight on a nearby table.

Here is how those three boxes interface with the list of sample items that could resurface in today's tickler file:

- The birthday card that needs to go in the mail today. Once the stamp is placed on it, throw it in "Out." When it is time to disperse the entire box, take the card and other mail to the main office and place in the school's outgoing mail.

♦ The tickets to tonight's concert. Put them in "Out," *or* go ahead and put it in a purse, wallet, or pocket.

♦ The driving directions for how to get to the concert. Throw in "Out," put in a briefcase, or possibly put in the purse or fold and put in a pocket.

♦ The folder of materials to discuss with Penelope's mom with whom you have a conference this afternoon. Place in "Pending."

♦ The phone message to call Mr. Jones. When you tried to call him last week, his secretary said he would be out of town until the 27th. Place the call immediately if convenient. If not, put a task in the "signature tool" to place the call and throw the message into "Pending" if the message contains some other information needed during the conversation. If the message simply contained the name and number, put the task in the signature tool and throw away the paper.

After having conducted countless workshops, participants tell me that instituting tickler files has made a significant difference in their ability to organize the paper in their lives. As a fellow practitioner, it is the tool that has allowed me to work with a clean desktop and a clear head my entire career.

Chapter 6 examines a second function for the tickler files. This second function also calls for a second label for each file. That point is clarified in the chapter.

The "Inbox," the "Mail Center" and Student Work

Teachers exist in a world where they receive paperwork from anywhere from 15 to 150 students on a daily basis. Having a system which minimizes time spent collecting, sorting, and returning papers is a huge time saver.

For the teacher, providing an "In" that students can access prevents interruptions. When a student has a note from a parent or makeup work to be turned in, where can they put them? Without clear direction, the answer will be to interrupt the teacher throughout the day to hand over miscellaneous pieces of paper.

One "In" may not be enough. Multiple letter trays allow teachers to pre-sort items. By using a different letter tray for each class period, having a designated letter tray especially for makeup work, or having or a tray strictly for absence notes and other correspondence from home, students placing the paperwork in the correct tray sorts the items.

My ninth grade English teacher, Betty Smith, had the most well-organized set of multiple Inboxes I have ever seen. Her system consisted of a freestanding cabinet with double doors on the front. Inside the cabinet were several shelves. On each shelf sat several letter trays. In the back of the cabinet were slots cut corresponding to the position of the letter trays. Each slot was labeled with exactly what was to go in it. Mrs. Smith had the cabinet turned so that one of the sides was against the wall. She had access to the double doors on the front. Students had access to the slots on the back.

An important element is that students have access to "In," in whatever form it takes, as soon as they enter the room. Papers are placed in the appropriate "In" before the students take their seats, eliminating time spent collecting papers.

Another idea recognizes the fact that papers should be placed in the order in which the names appear in the grade book in order to speed grade entry. As an early childhood teacher for more than 20 years, Pattie Thomas used a numerical sorter to accomplish this end. The device features strips of cardboard or plastic stacked on top of each other and secured at one end. Each strip is slightly shorter than the one below it. The end of each strip is labeled with a number. Each student in the class was assigned a number at the beginning of the year. Each time a child turned in an assignment, he or she placed the paper under the correct numbered strip on the sorter. Mrs. Thomas remarked that she could tell at a glance which students did not have an assignment. More importantly, when she slid the papers out of the sorter, they were already in grade-book order.

Just as collecting papers is a procedure that is repeating multiple times every day of the school year, returning student work is an equally regular occurrence. A good system saves time every day while a poor one serves as a daily time sink. For the elementary teacher, a "mail center" provides an efficient way to return papers. The system simply involves a cabinet or other devise which allows a cubbyhole or pigeonhole for each student. Papers to be returned and new papers to be distributed are placed in the student's "mailbox." This procedure works especially well for the student who is absent. Anything that has been missed during the absence awaits the student upon the return to school.

Reference Files Are Different

Discussions to this point in the chapter have centered on *action* items. Each piece of paper prompts us to *do* something. This portion of the chapter examines a system for handling reference information. We do not know when or if we will need the information again. The important element is that if we need it, we can find it quickly.

A–Z Files

Somewhere between action items and true reference items lies material to store for the short term. How often do you receive paperwork which probably will never need to be looked at again, but yet are not comfortable with throwing away? A flyer for a workshop comes in the mail. You are not interested in going, but just as soon as it is thrown away, your colleague will ask about the information for that very workshop. A student presents a letter from his parent, Mr. Smith. You make the phone call or do whatever else the letter asks. No further action is required, and it is probably the only letter Mr. Smith will send all year. Creating a file folder for one letter seems a waste. What do you do with this type of information? What sort of system can be devised so that such information can be filed very quickly and found again with little trouble?

I devote one filing cabinet drawer to this type of material. The file drawer contains 26 hanging file folders labeled A–Z. The letter from Mr. Smith goes in the *back* of the "S" folder. The flyer for the Acme workshop goes in the back of the "A" folder. If there are a few people who send numerous pieces of communication, those people can be given their own folders. One example might be the principal, Mr. Jones, who will likely send written communication to teachers throughout the year. Just behind the "J" file, would be a file labeled "Jones."

Why file to the *back* of the folder? Stanford University conducted a study that found that 87% of filed papers were never looked at again. Every piece of paper put in the A–Z files is a piece of paper that is not anticipated to be needed ever again. This system holds onto them "just in case." For this reason, the desirable filing system is one that takes *no time* to file. Putting the "Smith" letter in the back of the "S" file takes two seconds. Trying to keep the "S" file in alphabetical order, filing the letter between "Sk" and "Sn," would slow down the process.

For those times when papers need to be retrieved from the A–Z files, you will know which file to access. The next step is to think in terms of approximately *what time of year* the item arrived. Items from the first of the year will be found towards the first of the folder. Anything that came towards the middle of the year will be towards the middle of the folder. Within each file, therefore, papers are filed *chronologically* rather than *alphabetically*.

One of the repeating summertime tasks is to purge the set of A–Z files. By that time, you will have a solid idea of what truly can be thrown away and what is potentially of lasting value. Stack the entire set on the desk, open the "A" folder and look at each piece of paper for roughly one second. In that one second, make a decision to either "trash it" or "keep it forever." All of the "trash" items go in one stack. All of the "keep" items go face down in another stack. By the time you have finished the exercise, the "keep" pile is will likely be surprisingly thin. The "trash" pile may stand several feet tall.

At that point, take one file folder, label it "Correspondence [*fill in year*]," place the "keep" pile in the folder, and file the folder in the reference system. As for the other pile, shred sensitive items, and then dump the rest in a large recycling container. The A–Z set is now empty and ready for a new school year.

Long-Term Reference Files

Teachers accumulate a wealth of teaching materials during their careers. No matter how wonderful the material is, it is of no value if it cannot be found when it is needed. Setting up a tickler file is quick and easy. Likewise, labeling a set of folder A–Z can be done in a few minutes. Setting up a good reference filing system, however, is more difficult because it is going to require a great deal of planning. A good system will make filing logical and retrieval easy.

If you are new to the school, do not be surprised if you find overstuffed filing cabinet drawers, many unfiled papers, and a filing system that defies logic. On the other hand, you may be an experienced teacher who has created this mess and are reading this book in hopes of finding a way out.

Rather than simply trying to work with what has been left, do not be afraid to empty the entire contents of the filing cabinets onto the floor and start from scratch. The starting point is a logical filing system. These basic principles serve as a foundation for setting up and maintaining a long-term reference files:

- ♦ If space is at a premium, use manila file folders instead of hanging files. They take up far less room. This advice may seem to contradict the use of hanging files for tickler files and A–Z files. In both of those areas, not only papers, but entire manila folders are placed in them.

- ♦ Use a noun to begin the file name.

- ♦ Use broad category names.

- ♦ Use subheadings to break down the broader categories. Examples: Assessment—Math; Assessment—Science; Assessment—Writing. This arrangement will keep all assessment scores together. Files labeled "Math," "Science," and "Writing" would be spread out in various parts of the filing cabinet.

- ♦ Examine the contents of the files annually. While the system is designed for documents of long-term value, at some point certain material will outlive its usefulness.

♦ For files in which no additional material will be added and that are rarely accessed, consider storing them in another area of the building.

Other teachers in the building may already have excellent reference systems established. Select a couple of teachers with reputations for being highly organized and ask to examine their setups.

Organizing curricular resources chronologically is an excellent idea. Sandra Hutchinson, a first-grade teacher from Seaside Elementary School (Torrance, California) sets aside two file drawers for thematic units arranged chronologically according to the school year. An additional four drawers are filled with books organized by month and corresponding to the theme being studied. Ms. Hutchinson arranges big books by the month. In addition, she maintains a box of poems in chronological order and pulls selections each week to match the theme being studied. Storage boxes hold bulk items. The label on each box reveals the month the contents will be used or the theme with which they will be used.

Secondary teachers can also use this chronological concept. Jen Brown taught French and Spanish in Draper, Utah. She maintained a file folder for each chapter in the textbook. The folder contained handouts for the chapter, overhead transparencies, and games pertaining to the contents of the chapter. Ms. Brown stresses that within each folder she kept another folder containing the masters used for making copies. In that way, the risk of handing out the master copy to students was avoided.

Once you have a set of folders labeled appropriately, then and only then can you begin to sort through the contents on what you have emptied onto the floor and begin to dispose of the trash and organize what is worth keeping.

A later chapter examines setting up a logical filing system on the computer. At that point, you will be asked to examine your paper filing system and create a *comparable* structure on the computer. Doing a good job with establishing this reference filing system for paper will make composing its digital companion easier.

Bulk Items

Having a "place for everything" includes more than paper. With each teaching unit, the teacher has three-dimensional material that must be stored and then easily retrieved when it is time to introduce the unit. Bulletin board materials and decorations for the various holidays must be stored. Finally, we all have those items which should go into *In*, *Pending*, or *Out*, yet are simply too large. We need a logical place to put them.

Tubs

Large plastic tubs are excellent for storing seasonal bulk items. An orange tub with a black lid holds all of the Halloween decorations. Another tub holds Thanksgiving materials. A green tub with a red lid holds Christmas materials.

When one season ends, all of the items related to it go in one tub. Another tub is pulled, and in it is everything needed for the next season. You never have to hunt single items and find places to store single items.

Milk Crates

Milk crates provide excellent storage for materials accompanying each teaching unit. Bulk items, file folders, and hanging files can go in the same crate. When the unit is completed, put everything back in the crate and put it back on the shelf for another year.

Empty Shelf or Cabinet

When paperwork arrives and needs attention at some future date, you already have a place to put it. Throw it in the tickler file. What if the item is bulky? A microscope needs repair and you plan to deliver it to the proper person on Friday. Where do you put it from now until that time? You have a box of books to donate to charity and plan to take them on Tuesday of next week. What happens to that box of books until then? A new box of books arrives. Normally, newly arriving paper would go into *In*, but this incoming box is too large. What now?

For each of these examples, a designated spot for bulk items needing some type of attention provides an answer. An empty shelf is a possibility. An empty cabinet will work nicely. To make this bulk holding area work, two factors must be in place:

1. The designated shelf or cabinet can *only* be used for bulk items needing some type of action. Do not let that spot *also* accommodate items which are to be stored there permanently. If used properly, that bulk storage spot will spend the majority of its time *empty*.

2. Some *trigger* must be present which sends you to that bulk storage spot. Putting a reminder on the to-do list for the appropriate day to deliver the books, take the microscope for repair, delivery the books to charity, or unbox the newly arrived set of books will prevent those bulk items from being forgotten.

Whether you are new to the teaching profession, new to the school, or simply want to turn over a new leaf and move from a state of chaos to the freedom of order, creating a system which provides a place for every type of paper or teaching material constitutes a tremendous first step. You now have a "container" into which you will create an environment free of clutter. You will create a classroom where you can put your hands on anything without the need to "hunt." The time invested in creating the system translates into time saved each and every day.

Offsite Storage

Storage space is normally at a premium in classrooms. Items that will seldom, if ever, be used should not be allowed to occupy prime real estate in the classroom. The Christmas decorations which will be used for three weeks out of the school year should not reside in a storage cabinet in the classroom while materials needed every day have no space. Neither should those seldom-needed items be stacked on top of cabinets extending to the ceiling if other options are available. None of us would allow our formal dining room at home to be cluttered with boxes sitting on top of the china cabinet. Nothing gives a classroom a cluttered look quicker than its perimeters being used for long-term storage.

"Offsite" storage removes those lesser-needed materials from the classroom and allows more room for what will be used each day. For some, storing the material at home in the corner of a large garage may be the answer. Other teachers may be lucky enough to adopt a partially empty storage closet near their classroom. Along similar lines, one may find a storage area that everyone else avoids like the plague because it is so crammed with junk. Spend a Saturday dejunking and reorganizing this area and claim the newly found space as your own.

Anyone who has worked for very long in education will attest that making friends with the school custodian pays huge dividends. This is the person who can likely point you to unused storage space in the school and help keep others from encroaching on "your turf."

Next Steps

+ Answer this question for yourself, "What is on your desk or lying around the classroom at this moment which should go in a tickler file?"

+ Select a place to house your tickler files. Do you have a file drawer in your desk? If not, do you have a filing cabinet you can access while still sitting at your desk?

- Secure forty-three folders, preferably hanging files. Do not label them yet. Chapter 6 examines a second function for your tickler files and a second label for each.

- Purchase a memo pad with some refills.

- Establish an *In*, *Out*, and *Pending*.

- Devise methods for both collecting and returning papers.

- Secure a set of twenty-six hanging file folders and label them A–Z.

- Clear a filing drawer and set up your A–Z file there.

- Examine your present long-term reference filing system. What needs to be thrown away? What files need to be moved to another location?

- Examine the filing system for any needed reorganization and relabeling. Consult with other teachers about the organization of their systems.

- Collect tubs, milk crates, or other containers to house bulk items.

- Identify a shelf or cabinet in the classroom for bulk items which are requiring some type of attention.

- If space is at a premium, and it usually is in the classroom, identify "offsite" storage space for seldom-used items.

- Make friends with the custodian. Trust me on this one. While you are at it, make friends with the school secretary and lunchroom manager. Trust me on those as well.

3

Your Signature Tool: Organizing Digitally

There's not enough time in the day. Our enemy is time, and technology is the only way [to combat that].

> — John Q. Porter (*District Administration Magazine*, June 2006)

In the 1980s, when desktop computers began to become standard tools in the business environment, "personal information manager" software soon appeared on the scene. These programs offered the ability to keep a calendar and to-do list on the computer. Repeating appointments could be entered one time and magically show up on all future dates. To-dos not completed today simply rolled over to the next day's list. The software also functioned as an electronic address book, eliminating the need for a Rolodex or rewriting a paper address book every so often.

The only problem with this arrangement was getting up from the computer also meant leaving behind one's calendar, to-do list, and address book. Keeping all of this information on the computer simply was not practical, because it could not be accessed from anywhere. Today, the scenario is different. Smartphones are commonplace, and their ability to synchronize with a desktop computer makes the potential for organizing digital not only practical, but relatively easy.

Why Do I Need a System?

In today's world, information comes from all directions. This point is especially true for the teacher who is new to the profession or has moved to a different school. In this new environment, *everything* seems unfamiliar and it seems as though everything must be done *now*. Stress and a sense of being overwhelmed quickly take hold.

A well-defined system handles the remembering for you. Be it a creative idea, a phone number, a task to be done, or a date to be saved, your system handles it. You decide when you want to be reminded. You earn the right to forget about it. Your system acts as an alarm clock, providing the reminder at precisely the future time you had requested.

Master this art, and others begin to see you as being in control, relaxed, and on top of your game. Fall down in this area, and you will find yourself constantly searching for information. With notes scattered across random memos pads, sticky notes, on backs of used envelopes, you can never be sure where you stand on any project. Trying to simply remember it all, you quickly become frustrated, and wind up being seen by others as not quite having it all together, and wind up spending far too much time and showing far too little gain in any area of your responsibilities.

What is a "Signature Tool"?

This chapter and the one that follows are about crafting and using a "signature tool." This tool will serve as the one place to trap any new appointment, task, or piece of information. This tool turns *forgetting* from being a bad thing to a well-deserved right. Once your signature tool traps the item, your brain can forget about it and move on to more productive, creative thinking. The term *signature tool* is used for an important reason. If used to its full potential, it will be with you wherever you are. Others will notice that it appears from your pocket or purse anytime you need to jot down a new commitment or check an existing one. Those who know you well will realize that when they see that tool appear, the new commitment about which the two of you are talking will not "slip through the cracks."

Why Should I Use a Digital Tool?

A digital system does not necessarily provide the answer for a disorganized person. Quite the contrary, digital systems compound the problem by providing more and fancier ways for the disorganized person to lose information.

Digital systems work for people who have at least some rudimentary system in place, yet they find their system is not keeping up with the workload. For the busy teacher, a digital system offers three distinct advantages:

1. *Portable*—The smartphone that fits comfortably into a pocket or purse can easily store more information than a row of filing cabinets sitting in the corner of the classroom.

2. *Searchable*—The search capabilities of the both the smartphone and desktop programs such as Outlook allow retrieval of information much more quickly than a paper system.

3. *Shareable*—When inform is in digital form, it can be pasted into a document, blog, or e-mail message quickly and easily.

This chapter explores a thought process to help you decide if a "digital signature tool" is the right decision for you. The chapter also provides a methodology for how to use this digital signature tool to organize your life. The marketplace offers a variety of makes and models of these tools, and each will be accompanied by an owner's manual outlining the basics of how to operate the device. What is sorely lacking is the *methodology* for how to use them. While each passing year will bring new models which offer more features, the strategies offered here will continue to be sound.

A Day in the Life...

Perhaps the easiest way to illustrate the advantages of organizing digitally is to shadow a teacher who does so. The following is a day in the life of Jennifer, a teacher at Anytown Elementary School. Jennifer's varied and extensive use of her signature tool may not be typical. Her day does, however, illustrate the many possibilities handheld tools offer.

5:30 A.M.	Jennifer normally awakens to her alarm clock, but somehow the alarm began to malfunction lately. Jennifer simply sets the alarm on her digital signature tool, and is awakened promptly at 5:30.
6:00 A.M.	Jennifer is about to walk out the door, and had all but forgotten today is "trash day." It is a good thing she had set a repeating alarm to remind her to roll the trash receptacle to the curb.

6:10 A.M.	Jennifer is enjoying a leisurely breakfast. While she sips on a cup of coffee, she reads e-mail messages that have arrived since leaving school yesterday. Several messages are from a Internet discussion group for teachers to which she belongs. Jennifer finds this group to be an effective way to ask for input from colleagues around the country.
6:13 A.M.	The school chorus is traveling to a performance this morning, so Jennifer uses her signature tool to send the music teacher an e-mail wishing the group luck.
6:47 A.M.	After arriving at school, Jennifer boots her computer and plugs a cable into her signature tool. The few changes made on her handheld device since leaving her classroom yesterday are now synchronized with Outlook on her desktop computer.
6:51 A.M.	Jennifer looks at her task list. Because she tries to work ahead of deadlines, few tasks are urgent. Her aim is to organize the list so that like tasks are grouped together. The list is sorted by due date, so some creative reassignment of due dates groups her tasks. She assigns a due date of five days ago to several tasks she can complete before students arrive. She sees another half-dozen she can accomplish while students are coming in and starting their morning work. She assigns a due date of four days ago to them. A group of phone calls to be placed during her planning time will be next and receives a due date of three days ago. As each task is assigned a new due date, the task jumps to its new place on the list. She continues this process with the rest of the items on the list. Tasks she can handle while students are working independently are grouped together. Tasks that she will complete just after school are grouped together.
6:57 A.M.	Jennifer is now looking at a list of doable tasks for the day arranged in groups of similar items. She now has a plan for the day, and synchronizes with her signature tool once again, giving her the same organized tasks list on the handheld device.
7:30 A.M.	Jennifer uses this time before students arrive to talk briefly with the librarian, her principal, and two fellow teachers about upcoming events. Because the items are clear and grouped together, she is able to move through this part of the list quickly.

10:00 A.M.   An alert sounds on Outlook and Jennifer's handheld device. Although the students have no idea what the sound means, it is Jennifer's reminder that it is time for a particular student to take his daily medicine.

10:30 A.M.   The librarian had asked to see three of Jennifer's students at this time. Not trusting herself to remember during the middle of a lesson to send the students, Jennifer had set a reminder on Outlook. The chime reminds her to ask the students to go to the library.

11:00 A.M.   At lunch, a colleague asks Jennifer if she knows the dates that report cards will be sent home. Jennifer searches the calendar on the signature tool for "report cards" and in a matter of seconds has all of the dates in front of her.

1:00 P.M.   Planning time arrives. Jennifer leaves her class at the gymnasium. She takes out her signature tool and looks at the list of tasks she had planned for this point in the day. They include three phone calls and a visit with the librarian. One of the calls she places is an order for teaching materials. The receptionist asks for her account number. The contact list on Jennifer's signature tool has ample room to record such information. Jennifer is able to look up the account number during the call.

1:20 P.M.   Before picking up her class, Jennifer glances at the newspaper and sees the dates of upcoming symphony concerts. She is particularly interested in the "pops" concert coming up in a month. "I wonder if they have their program selections for that concert posted on the website," Jennifer thinks. She goes to the site and finds the complete list of selections which will be played, along with other details about the evening's performance. She clicks and drags the mouse to highlight all of the desired information and uses the "copy" command. Turning to Outlook, Jennifer enters the date of the concert on her calendar. She pastes all of the information copied from the website into the note section of that appointment. When she leaves from work today, all of that information will be available to her on her signature tool.

3:00 P.M.   Jennifer supervises bus dismissal. One of the buses is not in the lineup, so Jennifer makes a quick call to the principal from her signature tool.

3:20 P.M.   Jennifer stops by the textbook storage room to check for surplus books. The power goes out, and without windows in the storage room, Jennifer finds herself in total darkness. Jennifer pulls out her signature tool and presses a key. The light from the handheld provides enough illumination for Jennifer to find the door. "All of these features and it's a flashlight too!" she thinks.

3:35 P.M.   Checking her e-mail, Jennifer reads a request from her principal for some student data regarding her grade level. Jennifer knows that the teacher next door has already assembled that information, so she forwards this e-mail to the teacher and annotates it with a request that she share the information. Jennifer includes herself in the "bcc" line of the e-mail. The next time Outlook downloads e-mail, the copy that arrives in her Inbox serves as a reminder of the task she has delegated.

3:40 P.M.   Another e-mail advertises a free webinar. Jennifer is not sure if she wants to register, but wants to see the invitation again in a week. She drags the e-mail to her task list and assigns both a start date and due date a week from now. Jennifer can now delete the e-mail and forget about the invitation. A week from now, the invitation will show up on her task list. All of the details will be in a note attached to the task.

3:44 P.M.   Jennifer opens e-mail forwarded from the principal announcing a retreat for administrators. Since Jennifer is an aspiring administrator, she is being asked to come also. The message includes driving directions and outlines the agenda for the meeting. She uses Outlook's drag and drop feature to drag the e-mail to her calendar and adds a date and time. Before closing the appointment, Jennifer sets an alarm to remind her 30 minutes before the start time. Jennifer can rest assured she will not forget the meeting. The alarm on her signature tool will not allow it. When she gets in the car, the driving directions will be safely tucked away in a note attached to that meeting on her signature tool. The agenda will go with her, being stored in that same note.

3:50 P.M.	Jennifer's husband calls to tell her he has volunteered the two of them to become members of a supper club. It will meet at 6:00 P.M. the second Saturday of every month. As she listens, Jennifer enters the appointment into Outlook, clicks on "recurrence," selects "monthly" and "second Saturday" as the pattern. The supper club will now show up every month without another entry being made.
3:55 P.M.	Jennifer telephones the XYZ Company to place an order for several books. When the other party answers, she creates a new task on Outlook. In the note section, she puts the date and time of the call, the name of the salesperson and his extension. As he gives her the total for the sale, confirmation number, and date she should expect to receive the books, she adds that information to the note. When she hangs up, Jennifer completes the subject line of the task, "XYZ Company-3 books." She schedules a due date three weeks from now, corresponding to what the salesperson has told her. She changes the "status" of the task to "Waiting for someone else." She now saves and closes the task.
4:00 P.M.	Jennifer synchronizes her signature tool with Outlook once again. She walks out the door empty-handed, yet in her pocket is a very complete calendar, and organized task list, her entire address book, a wealth of reference material, the ability to make a phone call, and even a quasi-flashlight, all in one little tool.

This "day in the life" example has two purposes. First, for someone with no background in signature tools, the versatility of this tool becomes apparent. Jennifer's story may be the spark to motivate a novice to learn more about the capabilities. Second, for someone who is familiar with smartphones, Jennifer's day will likely provide ideas for their use.

Paper or Digital: Three Recommendations for Making the Choice

If you are contemplating moving from a paper system to a digital one, Jennifer's day illustrates many advantages of the latter. To help with making that decision, consider these three recommendations:

Experiment with a Smartphone

First, get the feel of smartphones by taking a trip to a local office supply store and a couple of cell phone retailers. The variety of models available and the ever-changing nature of the industry prevent offering any type of meaningful tutorial here. A helpful sales person will be able to show you how to navigate the device to add appointments or tasks. Also, any book superstore will carry books that explain how to work the device.

Experiment with the Desktop Software

Second, experiment with the software you will use to synchronize with the handheld device. Microsoft Outlook is so common that any handheld that has the capability to synchronize with any type of desktop software is going to synchronize with Outlook. Because Outlook is a standard component of Microsoft Office, the program is already accessible to most teachers.

Examine How Much Information Arrives Digitally

Finally, examine how much information arrives digitally. How many e-mails do you receive that include directions on how to get to a destination, agendas for meetings, confirmations of online orders, or requests from others to perform certain tasks? How much information do you acquire from the Internet? In each of these cases, printing the information to paper is one answer. The process, however, only makes the problem of the glut of paper in our lives that much worse. A much better alternative is develop a system which allows information which *comes* digitally to *stay* digital.

Appendix B provides detailed instructions on how to configure Outlook. The body of this chapter discusses the methodology of how to use Outlook and your signature tool. If you are new to Outlook, or if at any point some aspect of using Outlook is unclear, please refer to Appendix B for direction.

The Calendar

Keeping a calendar seems like such a simple idea, yet maintaining a calendar that is complete without being cluttered is an art. We must be able to look at the calendar and see at a glance what blocks of time are "set in stone." This kind of clarity is impossible when the calendar is littered with a variety of to-do items and random notes. At the same time, if there is not some place to write all of this other material, we begin to jot them on the first scrap of paper available or convince ourselves we can simply remember it all.

Three Types of Items Only

The calendar should display exactly three types of items:

1. *Appointments*—Assign a start and end time. Set an alarm if necessary. If the same appointment recurs regularly, enter that information. Use the note section to add details about the appointment. The announcement of the retreat for administrators from Jennifer's principal which was detailed in her e-mail is such an example (Figure 3.1). When synchronized to the handheld device, the appointment and all of the notes will transfer. Figure 3.2 shows the results of what will happen when the computer is synchronized to a handheld device. The icon to the right of the appointment shows that notes are attached.

Figure 3.1. Appointment with Information in Note Section

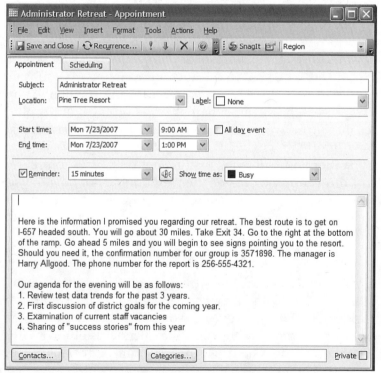

Figure 3.2. Appointment with Notes on Handheld Device

2. *Tasks that absolutely must be done that day*—Reserve time on the calendar and treat working on that task as you would any other appointment. If the grant proposal must be postmarked today and I have yet to finish the proposal, I will block out time on the calendar just as if it was an appointment. In addition, teachers may need audible reminders during their class time regarding *immediate deadlines*. With a digital system, setting appointments with alarms provides an *intentional* interruption.

3. *Events and activities which should be known about the day*—If no particular time is associated with the event, make it an "All-Day Event" as explained in Appendix B. The All-Day Event handles such situations as these:

   ◆ School holidays. For holidays that extend beyond a day, create one All-Day Event and simply indicate the start and end date. The event banner will appear on each day included in the range.

   ◆ Ending dates of grading periods or dates report cards are to be sent.

   ◆ Standardized test date windows. These time frames are published statewide more than a year in advance. Having them on the calendar helps greatly when planning the school year.

   Outlook also provides the capability of double-clicking on an All-Day Event and adding extensive notes. For example, the school's professional development days can be marked on the calendar. As plans are finalized for those days, record the details by double-clicking the All-Day Event banner and recording the details for the day (Figure 3.3).

Why not put other things on the calendar? If we mix what is critical with what is optional, we can no longer see what is critical. When an opportunity arises, you must be able to take one look at your calendar and say "yea" or "nay." We cannot do that if the three critical items are mixed in with the fifty-seven that are not.

Figure 3.3. All-Day Event with Notes

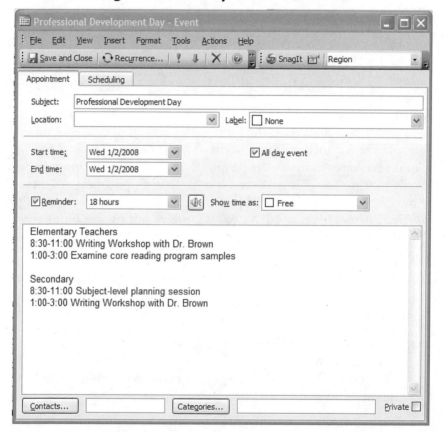

A History of Your Life

An additional use for the All-Day Event is to record major accomplishments of the day. What history-making event occurred today? What milestone occurred in your personal or professional life? Recording these types of events provides a permanent record of the most significant happenings in a person's life and time. This use of the calendar is discussed further in the next chapter. In addition, the "How Did You Make Today Count" section in that chapter is designed to help you add focus to your day and add to the pleasant memories your calendar can bring.

The Power of Reminders

The last section mentioned the need for reminders during class time of "immediate deadlines." Johnny needs to take medicine every morning at 10:00. How is the teacher supposed to handle something like that? Write a reminder on a sticky note and place it on the corner of the desk? Jot something in her plan book and hope she happens to be looking at it at 10:00? On the other hand, what if she could enter a reminder on her electronic calendar and instruct it to give an audible reminder at exactly 10:00? What if she could program that reminder *one* time and receive that audible reminder *every* weekday at 10:00? We have just uncovered one of the tremendously helpful advantages of a digital signature tool.

Teachers get involved in their lessons. They get involved with their students. Not letting "time get away" can be a real challenge, especially for the new teacher. Who would not welcome a little reminder five minutes before time to line up for lunch, especially on those days when the lunch schedule has been shifted because of an assembly program? A little chime five minutes before time to line up certainly beats a call from the office five minutes *after* the class should have already been in the lunchroom! Because a digital signature tool can issue an audible reminder, the savvy teacher delegates the job of remembering to the tool, while she devotes her attention to the more creative aspects of the job.

Other Calendar Views

One advantage of a paper month-at-a-glance calendar is that it allows one to see the "big picture." A day-at-a-glance version provides room to write details. The Outlook calendar provides both views. The user is not forced to choose between one or the other as with the paper calendar. On the toolbar, buttons allow users to see the five-day work week, the seven-day week, or the entire month. The ability to toggle between the one-day view and the monthly view provides a significant advantage for the busy teacher who must balance the "big picture" and the small details.

Smartphones also allow the user to switch between a view of the day, the week, or the entire month. Many also provide my favorite—the "Agenda View." This view provides a simple, continuous list of all calendar events.

The month view uses dots to show the approximate position of appointments during the day—morning, afternoon, and evening. Figure 3.4 shows a month for which the third has an appointment in the morning, the seventh has appointments in the morning and late afternoon, and the fourteenth has appointments covering all portions of the day. At a glance, it is clear what days are open for appointments and which days are already committed. Clicking on any day immediately displays a detailed view of that day.

Figure 3.4. Appointments in Monthly View

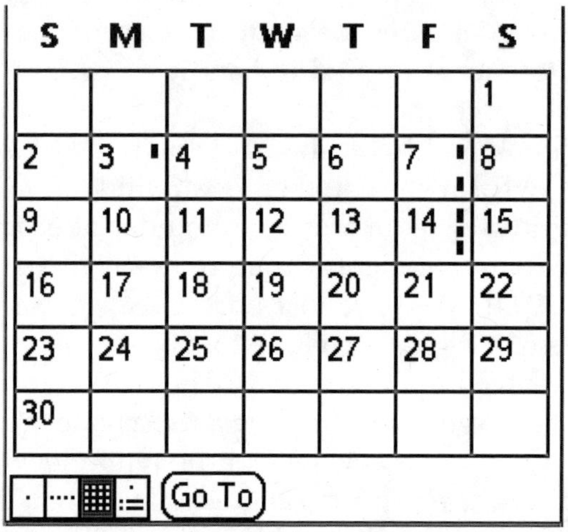

Navigating the Calendar

Those who criticize users of digital systems often point to the time needed to navigate to a particular date. If asked what is on one's calendar for a date six months out, the person who uses a paper calendar flips six pages over and is now looking at the date in question. For many digital users, however, navigating the calendar is cumbersome.

I currently use a BlackBerry smartphone and set the "Agenda View" as my default. If asked to look at a date six months out, I do the following:

1. Click the left-hand convenience key, which I have programmed to go directly to my calendar. I would now be looking at the list of events for today.

2. Press the letter "M." I will now be looking at the monthly view, such as what is shown in Figure 3.4.

3. Press the space bar six times. Each time I push the space bar, I am advancing one month. Pressing the key six times takes me six months into the future.

4. Roll the track ball to the date in question and press the "A" key. I am now back on the Agenda View and looking at the day in question.

Different models of smartphones will operate differently. Each, however, will have its shortcuts that make navigation easier. This point is important, because we tend to do what is easy. If certain functions of the smartphone are cumbersome, we soon cease to use them.

Purging and Printing

Every few months, print the Outlook monthly view for the last several months. This practice provides a "bird's-eye view" of one's life. On these calendars, restrict what is included to the major events and dates that are significant personally, professionally, or from a historical standpoint. For this reason, routine repeating appointments or meetings that held little significance would be deleted before printing. Minutes from those meetings are recorded elsewhere anyway.

The perfect time to review the calendar, delete the insignificant, and polish the important is during waiting time. When waiting in a checkout line, in a doctor's office, or when stopped by a train, editing past days on the handheld calendar puts wasted time to work.

An Organized Task List

The real "meat" of this system is the *organized task list*. Imagine for a moment a "to-do" list that never requires rewriting. Imagine being able to record a task just one time and seeing that task reappear each week, each month, or each year without having to enter another thing. Imagine a "to-do" list where any item can be opened to reveal a world of background information. Finally, imagine a list that is easily searchable, allowing you to find any item in seconds. The Outlook TaskPad is just such a tool. Many models of smartphones provide this function. Appendix B provides details on how to structure the Outlook TaskPad for this system.

Make the Next Step Crystal Clear

Examine your own list. How many of those items will really take a number of steps to complete? How many lack all of the information necessary to accomplish them? How many of the tasks are simply ambiguous and leave you at a loss to where to begin? When someone looks at a list and sees two items—a difficult one and an easy one—human nature dictates choosing the easy one. "Buy shoestrings" will win out over "solve world hunger" every time because we know exactly how to go about buying shoestrings. Solving world hunger, like so many other goals we may have, is large and undefined. We really do not know where to begin.

Figure 3.5 is an example of a list where clear tasks are intermingled with goals that would require multiple steps. Figure 3.6 is a list that actually stands a chance of being accomplished.

Figure 3.5 Unclear Task List

Supplies?
Improve math curriculum
Grant proposal
Maintain computer
Orders??
Get summer school going

Figure 3.6 Crystal-Clear Task List

Mills-Express interest in teaching summer school
Carter-Schedule observation
Report problem with heat
Acme 555–8312 check on status of order
Register for math workshop 555–7646
Research sources for technology grant
Outline ABC report
Compose blog post on use of ALEX

What makes the tasks in Figure 3.6 "crystal clear?" They possess the following characteristics:

♦ Crystal-clear tasks include verbs. Verbs are the *doing* part of speech. Read a crystal-clear task and you know exactly what it is you are supposed to do. Clarifying what is to be done on the front end increases the chances that you will know what to do when you see that task on the list later in the week.

♦ Crystal-clear tasks can be accomplished in one sitting, and ideally can be accomplished in a few minutes. Overly burdensome tasks tend to sit idle on lists whereas those that are easy to do get done. The trick is to break big jobs into tasks that are small enough that they are accomplished in a short period of time.

♦ Crystal-clear tasks have all needed information at hand. If the task is a phone call, the crystal-clear task has the phone number already written down. The agenda for the phone call is already written out.

♦ Crystal-clear tasks can be done *now*, without something else having to happen first. If something else must happen first, *that* is the task that needs to appear on the list.

Group Similar Items by Using "Due Dates"

Much has been written about arranging tasks by priority and working on high-priority items first. Certainly, we all have tasks that are critical to accomplish today whereas others can wait. Over the long haul, however, concentrating on the few critical items and ignoring everything else eventually results in a large backlog of tasks.

The reality of our jobs is that much comes our way on a daily basis. The ability to handle large numbers of fairly small tasks is essential. In many cases, other people require our approval or input in some way before they can move forward on a project. If we are focused only on a few critical items, the danger is that we become a huge bottleneck and hinder the productivity of those around us.

To accomplish a large number of tasks as quickly as possible, group similar items and handle the whole group at one time. For example, rather than interrupt a colleague with a question, start a list of items to discuss with that person, and run through the entire list during a single sitting. Rather than drive across town for one errand, start a list. When the list is long enough to make the trip worthwhile, run all of the errands in a single trip. One may need to have short interactions with a number of different teachers. List them all in one group and work through it just after the dismissal bell.

The birthday card example from the last chapter is a perfect example of grouping similar items. We bought all of the cards at one time, addressed them all in one sitting, and so forth, before dropping them into tickler files.

Suppose a teacher wants to encourage student participation in an upcoming event. One way this could be accomplished is to make an announcement over the public address system each morning, with each announcement unique and building in excitement to the day of the event. The project will flow more smoothly if the teacher blocks out some time and writes all of those announcements in one group. Once the entire series of announcements is written, each announcement is dropped into the appropriate tickler file.

How do you go about grouping related activities on Outlook or on a smartphone? The answer lies in using two techniques in tandem:

1. *Sort the list by due date.* One obvious advantage is that items that are overdue sort to the top of the list.

2. *Identify items that go together well and give those items the same due date.* Select several items that can be handled quickly upon arrival at school and assign them all a due date of around five days

ago. These items now appear at the top of the list. Identify several items that can be accomplished before students arrive and assign them all a due date of two or three days ago. Items you want to handle during your planning time could be assigned yesterday's due date. After school, you can work on a group showing today's due date. If the day is going well, you could even work on tasks showing tomorrow's due date.

Figure 3.7 shows an example of an organized task list on Outlook. Figure 3.8 (page 39) shows a similar list on a handheld device.

Figure 3.7. Organized Task List in Outlook

✓	!	TaskPad	S.	Due Date	S...	N...	↻
		Click here to add a new Task					
☐		Write recommendation for Cameron	T.	Tue 5/1/2007	N...		
☐		PDWeb-Approve outstanding requests	T.	Tue 5/1/2007	N...		
☐		PDWeb-Monitor signup for Tim	T.	Tue 5/1/2007	N...		
☐		DC-How many licenses do we need for HTM ...	W	Wed 5/2/2...	N...		
☐		DC-Has money been approved for math inte...	W	Wed 5/2/2...	N...		
☐		DC-Status of order for student response sys...	T.	Thu 5/3/2007	N...		
☐		John-Discuss order for student response sys...	F.	Fri 5/4/2007	N...		
☐		John-Discuss rollover on STI program	F.	Fri 5/4/2007	N...		
☐		Blog-Post info on field day at elementary sch...	S.	Sat 5/5/2007	N...		
☐		Blog-Post info on Riley scholarship	S.	Sat 5/5/2007	N...		
☐		Balanced scorecard-Cut/paste summary of w...	S.	Sun 5/6/2007	N...		
☐		Balanced scorecard-Add DIBELS scores	S.	Sun 5/6/2007	N...		
☐		Ellis-Bailey-Any negative comments on math ...	M.	Mon 5/7/2007	N...		
☐		Ellis-Examine documentation for School Impr...	M.	Mon 5/7/2007	N...		
☐		Ellis-See counselor re: 7th grade orientation	M.	Mon 5/7/2007	N...		
☐		Ellis-Borrow software for interactive whitebo...	M.	Mon 5/7/2007	N...		
☐		JP-Call to set date to review writing continuum	T.	Tue 5/8/2007	N...		
☐		Set dates for SACS planning meetings for th...	T.	Tue 5/8/2007	N...		
☐		Set date to compose science pacing guides	T.	Tue 5/8/2007	N...		
☐		Jones-Borrowed 3 books	F.	Fri 5/18/2007	W..		

**Figure 3.8. Organized Task
List on a Handheld Device**

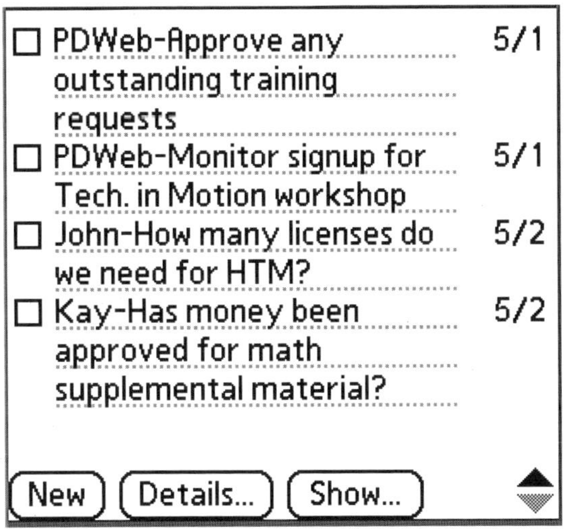

```
┌─────────────────────────────────┐
│ ☐ PDWeb-Approve any        5/1  │
│   outstanding training          │
│   requests                      │
│ ☐ PDWeb-Monitor signup for  5/1 │
│   Tech. in Motion workshop      │
│ ☐ John-How many licenses do 5/2 │
│   we need for HTM?              │
│ ☐ Kay-Has money been        5/2 │
│   approved for math             │
│   supplemental material?        │
│                              ▲  │
│ ( New ) ( Details... ) ( Show...) ▲│
│                              ▼  │
└─────────────────────────────────┘
```

Make Tasks Disappear and Reappear Using Start Dates

Some tasks cannot or should not be accomplished until a future date. Teachers constantly think of tasks needing attention during the following semester or summer. Certainly, one would not want these items, which will not require action until far in the future, to clutter the list for today. By simply setting a start date for sometime in the future, those tasks are out of sight for now. They will magically show up on the dates specified long ago.

The "Fab Five"

Each day identify the five items that will pay the biggest dividends and use them to provide focus for the day. Assign each of the five a due date several days in the past so that they move to the top of the list. As the day unfolds, those five tasks remain front and center.

Plan Weekly

Use the entire week as a canvas on which to create the following week. Too many people use tomorrow's list to house a month's worth of tasks. With each passing day, one seems to be getting further behind. At some point, we must gain a sense of just how much we can reasonably accomplish in a day and structure a list of that length.

Pick a day of the week when it will be convenient to run errands and assign errands that due date. Select a planning period one day to make a block of low-priority phone calls. As other low-priority calls come to mind, give them that due date. Select a day to meet with the principal, and perhaps even get on the principal's calendar. Throughout the week, assign items for that meeting. In a few minutes, you can cover a great deal of ground. Much time will be saved over trying to gain access multiple times during the week to discuss a single point here or there.

Work Ahead of Deadlines

When we are able to group similar tasks, those tasks are accomplished much faster than attacking them any other way. The greatest single enemy of this approach consists of working too close to deadlines. When deadlines loom, our days are driven by whatever project is about to crash. Those who have experienced waiting too long to complete an application or request a purchase order have experienced what happens when the day is deadline driven. One winds up spending the better part of a day "walking" paperwork through its various steps, interrupting other people to ask them to act on the emergency, and experiencing a great deal of unneeded stress. On the other hand, the exact same paperwork initiated a week ago would have required virtually no amount of time. The paperwork would wind its way through the pipeline while the person requesting it spends time making headway on a variety of other projects.

The focus of *today* must never be to simply complete what must be done *today*. The organized teacher stays ahead of the curve. If a project begins to bog down, enough time has been built in to compensate. Orders are placed with vendors so that they arrive in plenty of time. Tasks are delegated to others far enough in advance that the people to whom we delegate need not immediately drop their other initiatives to work on the new assignment. Moving from a feeling of just keeping one's head above water to a feeling of being well ahead of deadlines may take putting in extra time for a while. The process also entails taking a hard look at the list for things which can be postponed until much later as well as things that need not be done at all.

Delegation

When a teacher delegates a task to someone else, it is important to have the capability to follow through and see that the task is completed. Outlook provides a field called "Status." One choice in that field is "Waiting for someone else." Changing the status of the task and assigning a due date will bring that task back to the user's attention on the due date. It is also easy to see a list of all of the tasks where someone else holds responsibility. Simply click the header on the "Status" column, and "Waiting for someone else" tasks will be grouped together on the list.

Searching the List

The organized task list drives the day. Items are assigned due dates such that the list "flows" with items that go together well. What happens, however, when you want to put a finger on a task and are not sure where it appears on the list, or if it appears at all?

Figure 3.9 shows the task list on a BlackBerry smartphone. Three items on the list involve "Jim." The due date assigned to those tasks ensures that those items will be in front of me on precisely the date I had decided I wanted to see them. Those tasks serve as the "trigger" to pick up the phone and call Jim or make a trip to see him. Keep in mind that other items pertaining to Jim may be further down the list and scheduled for future dates.

Figure 3.9. Searching for a Task on a Handheld Device

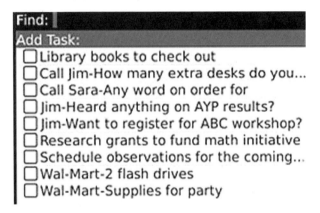

What if Jim comes walking in the door unexpectedly? Wouldn't I want to go ahead and discuss with him any of the items on the list even if they did not come due for several days? How can I quickly see a list of all items pertaining to Jim? A strong feature of the BlackBerry smartphone task list is the search feature. When Jim walks in the door, I would do the following:

1. Press the right-hand convenience key on the handheld, which is programmed to go immediately to the task list.

2. Start keying in the word "Jim."

As I press the keys, the task list is being filtered to only the items with the combination of the letters "Jim." I am now looking at a list of the items pertaining to Jim, regardless of the due date. The items will appear in the order they come due.

How would I accomplish this same skill set on Outlook? When Jim appeared, I would do the following:

1. Click the "Task" button on Outlook.

2. Enter "Jim" in the search window and click "Find Now."

The list, regardless of its length, would show all of the tasks involving Jim, and show them in the order they come due. Figure 3.10 (page 42) shows the list before filtering.

Figure 3.10. Searching for Tasks in Outlook

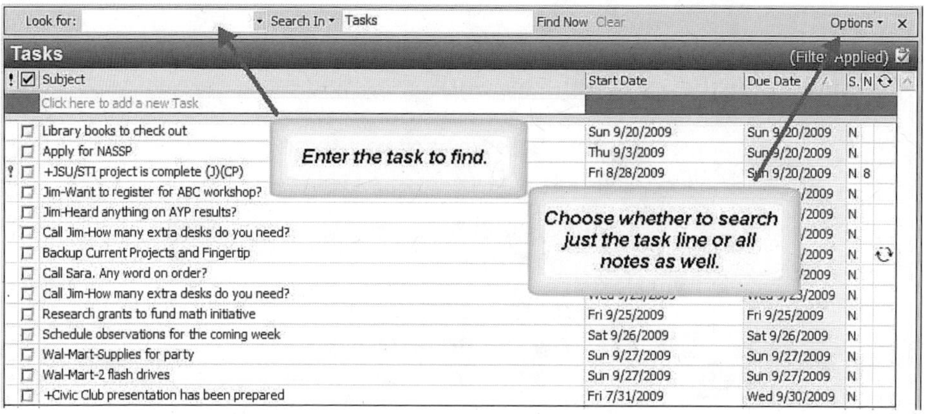

Documentation Made Simple

In a digital system, the note section of a task is the place for documentation. When Jennifer telephoned the XYZ Company at 3:55, she opened a new task as soon as she picked up the telephone. She first entered notes from the conversation in the large block. Once the conversation was over, she had to decide what to do about the notes and when. At that point, she completed the subject line and due date (Figure 3.11, page 43).

Keeping Digital Information Digital with Microsoft Outlook

In today's world, the teacher receives a flood of information via e-mail. A large part of staying afloat involves organizing digital information in a digital fashion. The "drag and drop" feature of Outlook allows us to turn an e-mail into an appointment.

Figure 3.11. Documenting a Phone Call

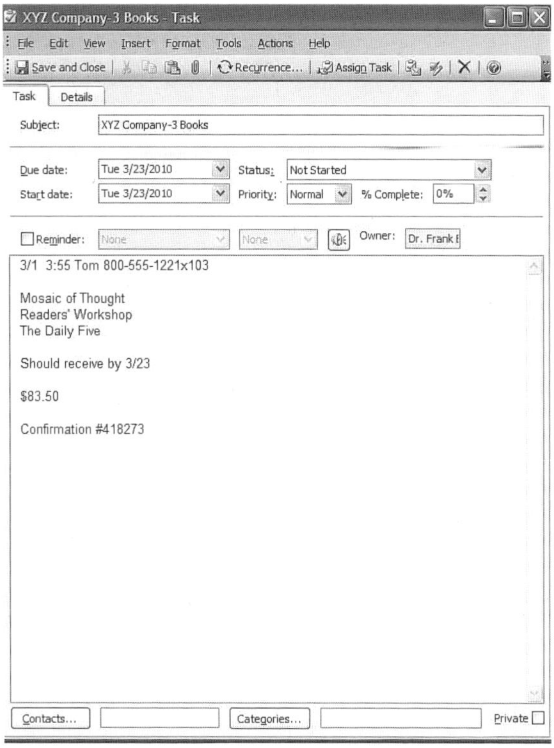

Drag and Drop E-Mails to Make Them Appointments

At 3:44, Jennifer handled an e-mail from her principal announcing a re-treat. Rather than print the e-mail and keep up with the printout of the driving directions and agenda, Jennifer chose to keep digital information digital. She closed the e-mail. She then clicked on the e-mail and proceeded to drag it over the Calendar button (Figure 3.12). As soon as she released the mouse button, Outlook opened a new appointment. We actually saw the results of this action on Figure 3.1 (page 30). The subject of the e-mail automatically populated the subject line of the appointment. The body of the e-mail was duplicated in the note section of the appointment. All Jennifer had to do was set the date, set the time, and save the appointment. She can now delete the e-mail.

Figure 3.12. E-Mail Being Dragged to Calendar Button

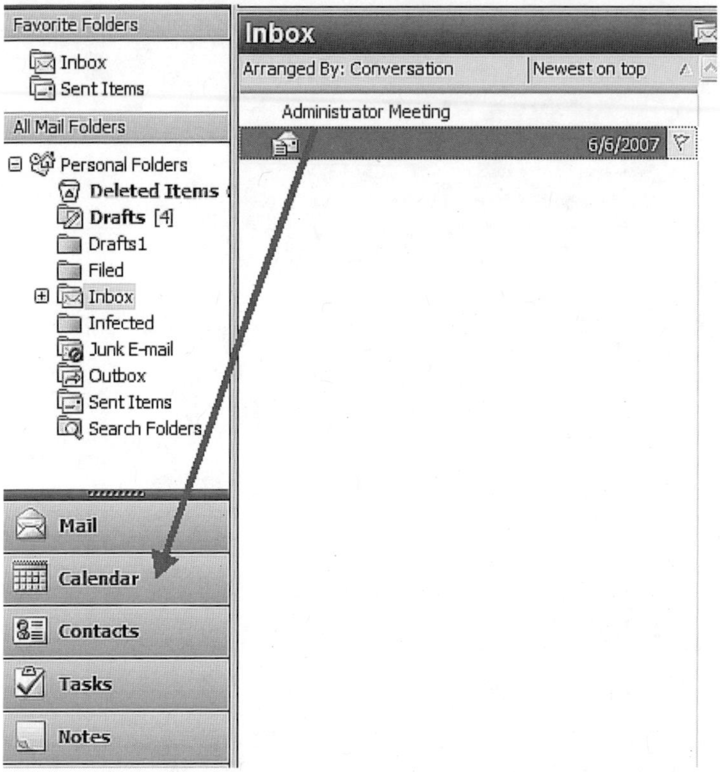

The whole process takes only a few seconds and does not require writing or printing anything. The next time the handheld device is synchronized with Outlook, this retreat, complete with the agenda and driving directions, will be copied to the handheld.

When the time approaches to leave for the retreat, an alarm sounds both on Outlook and on the handheld device as a reminder just in case Jennifer is preoccupied. Not sure how to get to the destination? The directions, which were originally a part of the e-mail, are on the handheld in a little note attached to that appointment. Likewise, the retreat agenda, which had also been part of the e-mail, is part of the note attached to that appointment.

Drag and Drop E-Mails to Make Them Tasks

Many an e-mail embeds a "to-do." We can "drag and drop" any e-mail and turn it into a task. During Jennifer's day, she received an e-mail inviting her to participate in a webinar. She really does not know at this point whether or not she wants to participate, but believes that within a week, she will be able to make a decision. Basically, Jennifer wants this information to go away and reappear in a week. She closed the e-mail and clicks and drags the e-mail over the Task button (Figure 3.13). Outlook opens a new task (Figure 3.14). The subject of the e-mail automatically populates the subject line of the task. The body of the e-mail is duplicated in the note section of the task. All Jennifer has to do is set the start and due dates and save the task. She can now delete the e-mail.

Figure 3.13. E-Mail Being Dragged to Task Button

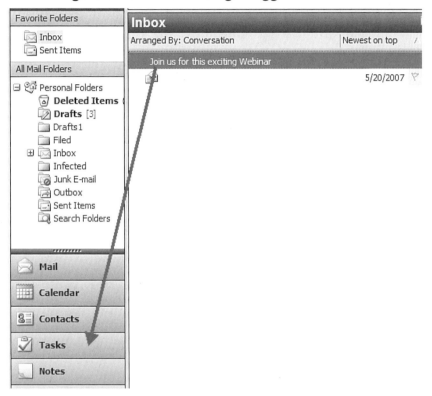

A Very Complete Contacts List

"Contacts" in Outlook is the substitute for the paper address book you find yourself rewriting every couple of years. Figure 3.15 (page 47) shows the elements at one's command for any contact. In addition to the fields for a host of information, Outlook provides a large section for notes. The information you might include in this note section includes:

♦ Directions on how to get to that person's house or business.

♦ Clothing sizes for relatives.

♦ Names of your friends' children and their birthdays.

♦ Your account number with a business.

Figure 3.14. E-Mail Text Displayed in Note Section

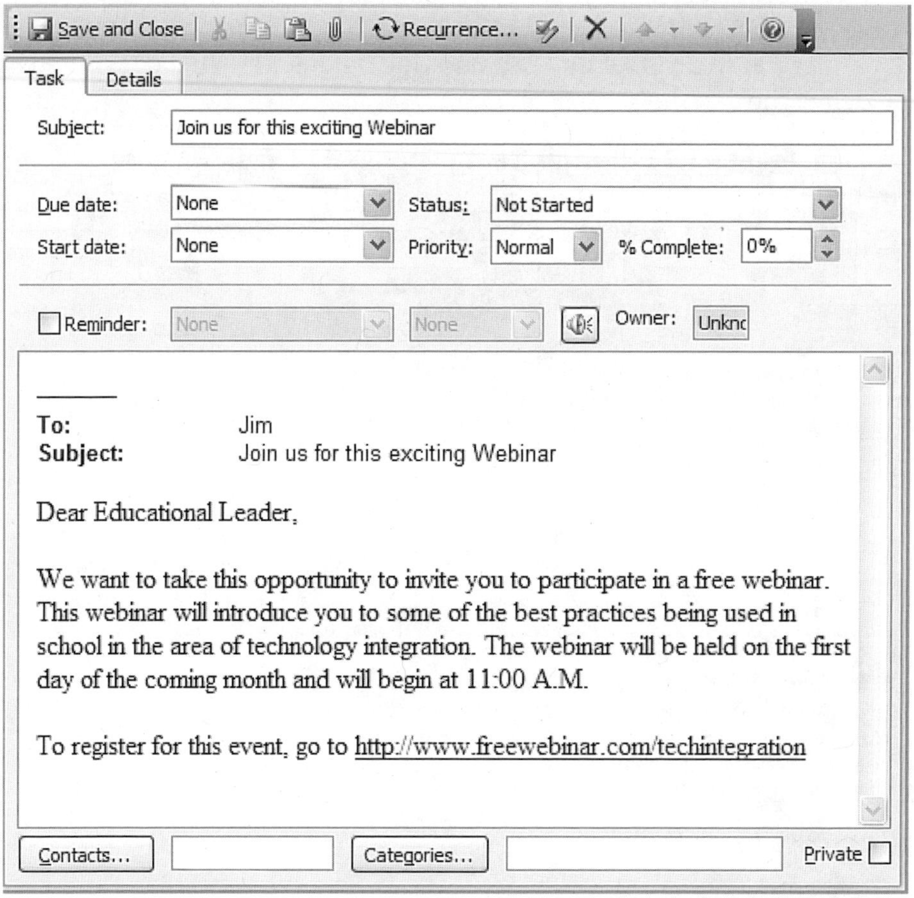

A Wealth of Reference Material

The Notes section of Outlook is a place where you can store reference information. Here are some examples of the information which could be kept in Outlook Notes.

♦ *Numbers*—One Note can hold all of the passwords for various websites, the school system's federal tax ID, the code for the photocopier, and the burglar alarm code, just to name a few. It is amazing how many numbers we are expected to be able to produce. This one note can hold all of them.

Figure 3.15. New Contact Record in Outlook

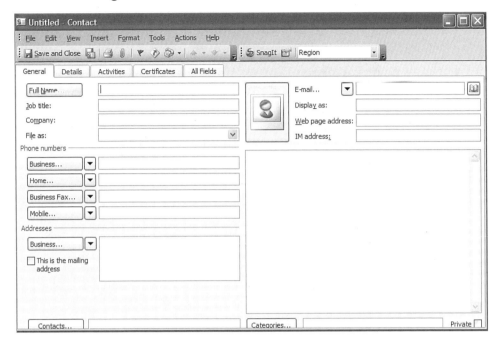

- *Checklists*—We all have certain activities that are composed of a number of steps. A set of checklists keeps us from "reinventing the wheel" countless times.

- *Documentation from calls and conferences*—At times, the notes taken while on the phone are valuable because of the content. Other times, we simply need to document what was said and agreed upon in case disagreements arise later. The drag-and-drop feature is valuable here. If a task on the list is "Call Mrs. Jones," then during the call, use the note section of that task to document important points from the call. If you feel those notes are of "lasting value" and want to retain those notes indefinitely, drag the task over the Notes button. Outlook automatically creates a new note. The program even date and time stamps the note.

- *Descriptions of each of the workshops one conducts*—If you conduct workshops or seminars, a brief description of each of them is a helpful piece of information to have at hand.

- *Devotionals, inspirational messages, and quotes*—As teachers, we are often called upon to offer a devotional or inspirational message or simply to "say a few words" prior to a meeting or meal. Usually these requests come on the spur of the moment. Having a few of these gems tucked neatly away in your "signature tool" comes in handy.

♦ *Data*—What are some of the significant facts and figures from the latest standardized test? What data could you site related to the progress of your classroom or school? When addressing parent groups or talking to the local news reporter, having some facts and figures handy pays big dividends.

♦ *Student list*—You will need a student "check-off" list countless times during the year.

♦ *Common documents, legislation, policies*—Would you like to have a copy of the Declaration of Independence at hand? Do you find yourself referring to a particular Board of Education policy or state statute often? Each of these is a candidate for a Note in Outlook.

What is the Role of Paper in a Digital System?

During my transition from a paper system to a digital one, the aim was to go totally digital. This approach worked well except for one area—documentation. During a phone conversation while seated at my desk, documenting in Outlook is easy. During a face-to-face conference, keying notes into a computer is out of the question. Likewise, entering data into a smartphone is too slow and would pose too much of a distraction. In meetings, taking notes directly into a smartphone is slow and would be mistaken for off-task behavior. In these situations, there is nothing like paper.

When I am in a meeting, at a workshop, or in a face-to-face conference, I take with me my paper journal. I do not have one journal for parent meetings, another for groups meetings, another for workshops which I attend, and so on. Instead, I have one journal for everything. The pages are labeled chronologically. If I know the date of the event, I can easily put my hands on the notes.

In the next chapter, the section on documentation using a paper planner illustrates how I use the journal. The "right-hand page" of the Day-Timer I used for a decade became the basis for the way in which I use my journal today.

The "Mother Ship" and the Satellite

The majority of our discussion has been a methodology for using Outlook at your desk, and for good reason. A command of Outlook is a precursor for establishing a complete system on the handheld device. Operating a keyboard with 10 fingers is far quicker and easier than entering information with two thumbs. "Heavy-duty entry" is going to be done in Outlook. It is helpful to think of the desktop computer as the "mother ship" and the handheld as a satellite. Synchronizing the handheld to Outlook, a one-minute ritual, is the first thing to do upon arrival at work and the last thing to do before going home in the evening.

I chose to use Outlook in my discussion of desktop software for three reasons:

1. Outlook is my program of choice. It is the software with which I am most familiar.

2. Outlook is the most popular software of its kind on the market today.

3. Trying to provide examples for a variety of different software packages would make the discussion unduly long. Users of other software will be able to take the concepts here and apply them to the software they are using.

Any handheld device comes with an instruction manual that explains the function of each button and the list of choices of each menu. Numerous books are devoted to operating instructions for specific devices. By intention, this chapter makes no attempt to duplicate what is already available through those venues.

What is almost universally neglected in those publications is any type of comprehensive system for organizing information and insuring that information appears at the right time and in the most helpful format. This chapter, along with the upcoming chapter on managing multiple projects, provides such a system.

Paper or digital? The decision for your "signature tool" rests as much with personal preference as anything else. You may have already made a decision. Perhaps that decision will be made as you work through the remainder of this book. That decision may even change over time as the complexity of your life changes.

Next Steps

◆ Reread Jennifer's typical day. How do you presently handle each of the scenarios described? What are the strengths and/or shortcomings of the system you presently use in terms of how you would handle each scenario?

♦ Schedule a trip to an office supply store or cellular phone provider and experiment with several of the smartphones.

♦ Experiment with Outlook. You could do so on your own computer or one located in a computer lab. You might try duplicating some of the examples in this chapter.

♦ For the next several days, pay special attention to the amount of information that comes to you digitally. How much of it are you printing? Of that, how much is useful only for a short time and is then discarded? How much is stored long-term? How and where is it stored?

♦ If your decision is to organize digitally, read Appendix B carefully and set up Outlook in the manner outlined there. Realize that all things improve through practice. You will make mistakes as you begin working with both Outlook and your digital signature tool. You will fumble. With time, you will flourish. The investment of a little time and patience will pay big dividends in the long run.

4

Your Signature Tool: Organizing With Paper

The master thinker knows that ideas are elusive and often quickly forgotten, so he traps them with notebook and pencil. He heeds the Chinese proverb: "The strongest mind is weaker than the palest ink."

— Wilferd A. Peterson in *Adventures in the Art of Living*

Let pencil and paper do your remembering. That statement provides the single greatest organizational and time management strategy that can be can offered. Be it an idea, a phone number, a task to be done, or a date to be saved, as soon as the thought arrives we must develop the habit of writing it down, or, as we saw in the previous chapter, recording it digitally.

This chapter is about designing and using a paper "signature tool." The concepts are the same as what we saw in the previous chapter. Only the tool is different. Whatever form one's signature tool takes, it is indispensable in a world where our commitments are great, our time is precious, and the consequences for "dropping the ball" can be costly.

Paper or Digital?

We live in a world that is increasingly digital. At the same time, paper continues to be a trusted medium. Should your system be paper- or electronic-based? Valid arguments exist for each camp. Paper requires no special tools. One does not have to learn any software. Input is effortless. A paper system is inexpensive. Finally, many people simply like the feel of paper.

Five Functions and Five Guiding Principles

Regardless of what tool we use, a signature tool must be able to perform five functions:

1. *Remind us of appointments.* Every calendar is capable of this function.

2. *Display our tasks (or "to-do" items).* In this area, most monthly calendars will be inadequate. The volume of tasks a teacher is expected to handle is simply too large to be housed on a monthly or even week-at-a-glance calendar.

3. *Remind us of tasks delegated to others.* The saying "no man is an island" is very true in education. We work with others on projects and depend on them to uphold their end. Parent volunteers commit their time and energies to our classrooms. Will they come through without any prompting? We order materials from a vendor. How will we keep track of what has been ordered, what has been received, and whether the billing is correct? Colleagues borrow books and other resources from us. How will we remember what we have loaned, to whom it has been loaned, and what has been returned? How can we keep track of everything *other* people are supposed to doing?

4. *Allow us to record and retrieve communication.* Teachers are told to "document." Topics discussed and decisions made during a parent conference may seem insignificant at the time, yet may be of great importance months later. Unfortunately, few teachers have been given any system for documenting quickly and later being able to retrieve information easily.

5. *Help us manage goals.* Good teachers set goals for themselves and their students. They also realize that accomplishing a goal involves organizing a whole series of tasks over a period of time and beginning to chip away at them one-by-one. The challenge becomes even greater when multiple goals come into play at the same time.

Regardless of the tool, five guiding principles are essential for any organizational system:

1. *Use only one system.* All calendar events, whether personal or professional should be placed on the same calendar. The person

who uses use two calendars can never be sure if the one being viewed is complete. In short, the person who uses two calendars cannot trust either one.

2. *The system must be portable.* It will go from school to home and back. It will go to faculty meetings and to the grocery store. If it is bulky, you will likely leave it on your desk.

3. *Keep the system handy.* The system is of little good if it is not with you.

4. *Get rid of scraps of paper.* Write it all in your system. We are tempted to grab the first Post-It note or back of an envelope to jot the thing we must remember. Fifteen minutes later, we cannot find the scrap of paper. Everything must go in the system.

5. *Let the system do the remembering.* We cause ourselves unneeded stress by trying to keep track of our varied responsibilities in our heads. When an obligation first comes to our attention, we must enter it in the system right then. It is a habit and one that must be developed. The reward is that when we enter something into our system, we can forget about it.

This chapter concentrates on three functions of the paper signature tool: (a) the calendar, (b) the task list, and (c) daily documentation.

Choosing a Signature Tool

The signature tool can take a variety of physical forms:

♦ *Day-Timer or Franklin-Covey planner.* These commercial planners offer two facing pages for each day. The left-hand page houses appointments and tasks. The right-hand page provides a place for the type of documentation we will discuss.

♦ *Loose-leaf binder or spiral notebook.* One can just as easily build a planner with the same two-page-per-day format as mentioned with the commercial planner.

♦ *Legal pad or steno pad.* One page can be devoted to each day. One section of the page is used to list calendar events, a second portion lists tasks, and a healthy lower half of the page is used for documentation.

♦ *Plan book.* For the teachers desiring one tool to house both lesson plans along with calendar and task items, a standard plan book is a viable option. In addition to the columns devoted to the various class periods or subjects, one column would be reserved for calendar items and one for tasks. The advantage this system offers is that events that would go on the calendar also impact lesson planning. Letting one form serve both purposes eliminates the need to copy the information in two different places. The downside is that the plan book made be too large to be taken everywhere.

♦ *Printout from a digital calendar.* This option offers a hybrid between a paper system and a digital-based system. Each day, print a page containing appointments and tasks. During the day, mark through tasks completed, and write in new tasks. Use the reverse side as a place for documentation. At the end of the day, update calendar and task information in the digital system. Establish a file folder for all of the old printouts. Their value will be the documentation they hold on the reverse side.

The tool can take many forms. What is important is using one tool and developing a solid strategy for keeping all commitments in that one place.

The Calendar

Whether we use a paper calendar or a digital one, we must be able to see our entries in two views: (a) month-at-a-glance, and (b) a daily or weekly view tied to our task list. The first allows for viewing the "big picture" and serves as an indispensable planning tool. The second provides the marching orders for *now*. Digital calendars allow the user to toggle between several views, as we saw in the last chapter. Those using a paper-based system will need to incorporate a simple month-at-a-glance calendar with the signature tool. My personal practice when I used a Day-Timer was to enter items straight onto the daily pages for any items coming up within the same month. Anything for a future month went on the monthly calendar. At the end of each month, I would transfer all of the items for the following month onto the daily pages.

What Goes on the Calendar?

To achieve clarity, limit calendar entries to three types of items:

1. *Appointments*—Obligations to be at a certain place at a certain time go on the calendar. Virtually everyone is already accustomed to these kinds of things. The conference with John's mother Tuesday at 3:00 and the dental appointment October 12 at 4:00 are examples.

2. *Tasks that absolutely must be done that day*—With a glance at the calendar, the owner can see that block of time is committed to

this urgent task and will not schedule another activity for the same block of time.

3. *Things that need to be known about the day*—The teacher across the hall is having a guest speaker in her class on Tuesday. The deadline for posting grades is Friday. The teacher next door will be having a substitute next Wednesday. Each of these pieces of information is specific to that day. Each might or might not impact actions we take during the day. At least, with these events on the calendar, we know the event is happening so that decisions can be made as time approaches.

Keeping the calendar clean allows that which is critical to stand out.

A History of Your Life

The month-at-a-glance calendar shows what is coming up in the future. It also has the potential to record the *significant* happenings of the *past*. Flipping ahead in the calendar, one is likely to see reminders of such events meetings, holidays, dental appointments, athletic games and practices. What do we see about the days that have passed? In all likelihood, we simply see an "X" marked through the day. This calendar offers an opportunity for more.

Use a pencil on that month-at-a-glance calendar, and do so for two reasons. First, events change. Parents call to reschedule conference times. Faculty meetings get cancelled. Scratching through events leaves a mess on the calendar. Erasing and rewriting with a pencil is easy and leaves a neat appearance.

Second, use a pencil so that at the end of the day you can erase that which was mundane and replace it with that which was significant. If you were to look back at the calendar for this year a year from now, is it important to see that you attended a faculty meeting? On the other hand, if you are a parent, and today was the day your baby took his first steps, how significant is that? Is that something you would like to see on the calendar when you look back a year or ten years later?

How Did You Make Today Count?

At the end of every day, I ask myself one simple question: "How did you make today count?" All too often, we experience successes during the day worthy of remembering later, yet fail to record them anywhere. The month-at-a-glance calendar provides the perfect place. What happened in your school, your family, your community, or your world today that you would like to be able to look back upon years from now? Add those items as well. Erase the mundane that was written in pencil and replace it with the significant, recorded in indelible ink.

A calendar managed in this way provides a history of your life, the events that were important in it, and takes no more than seconds per day. At the end of the year, your calendar will no longer go in the trash can. Instead, it will take prominent place on a bookshelf.

An Organized Task List

No one knows who originally thought up the idea of the "to-do" list. More than likely, as soon the first such list grew to more than about five items, the question arose, "How do I know which one to do right now?"

Every one of us certainly can generate a list of obligations we have that far exceeds what can be accomplished by the end of the day. Having some way to organize a laundry list of tasks into a doable "game plan" is the challenge.

Make the Next Step Crystal Clear

The organized task list on paper adheres to the same principles as its digital counterpart examined in the last chapter:

- Word tasks clearly.
- Group similar items.
- Plan the list on a weekly basis.
- Work ahead of deadlines.
- Use the "Fab 5" to add focus to the day.

If you use paper to plan, and perhaps neglected the previous chapter, the discussion on these five concepts applies equally well to both approaches.

The concept of weekly planning is even more critical in the paper environment. When a long list is written for today and 90% of those tasks are left undone and recopied for the again for the next day, the experience can be frustrating. Gaining a sense of what can reasonably be accomplished in a day and structuring a plan for the entire week are crucial elements.

Pick a day when it will be convenient to run errands and begin a list on the page for that day. As other errands come to mind, flip to that day and add to the list. When that day arrives, the list serves as the trigger to make those errands happen. Should you find yourself out and about on some other day, you know to where you can flip and see a collection of your errands. The same principle holds true with a block of phone calls you may want to make or items you wish to discuss with another person.

Delegation

From time to time, we assign a task to someone and want to be sure the other person comes through. We loan a book and want to be sure the book is returned. We order materials from a business and want to be sure that what we have ordered is delivered, that the order is correct, and that we have been charged the correct amount. Each of these scenarios is an example of delegation. The task belongs to someone else, yet we have a vested interest in the other person completing that task. How can we keep track of all of the tasks that belong to someone else?

The signature tool provides the answer. As soon as the assignment is made, as soon as the book is loaned, or as soon as the order is placed, a note goes in the signature tool. Delegated items can be classified items into three categories:

1. *Date specific*—The task must be completed by a certain day this week. For this type, flip to that day and make an entry. Part of one's responsibility when that day comes is to followup as needed on that task.

2. *No specific date, but should be completed within the next week*— I would certainly expect any phone message I leave to be returned within the week. The same exists for small tasks. Group these items together in a list. Friday may be a good day to check the status of all items of this type.

3. *Tasks that should be accomplished within the month*—An order placed may require several weeks for delivery. Reserve the page just behind the last day of the month in the back of the planner to list delegated items. Figure 4.1 shows a sample list. Notice the parentheses used beside two of the items. Their use will become clear in the next section as we discuss documentation.

Figure 4.1. List of Delegated Tasks

```
Adams—Borrowed Excellence in Teaching book
Cooper—Minutes from grade-level meeting
Acme—Order #18762 (4/12)
Smith—Update on Billy Jones (4/21)
```

Documentation Made Simple

Every first-year teacher has been told documentation is important. Countless times during our careers, we are reminded to *document*. How many of us, however, have really been taught how to document? Exactly what is it that we are supposed to document? How do we know what is important and what is not? Where do we document?

In practice, very few people have a good ongoing system of documentation. The key element for a person to document on a regular basis is that the system must be *easy*.

During my early years in education, I tried various approaches to documenting such tasks as telephone calls to parents, all without much success. No matter what I tried, the paperwork involved was just enough trouble to cause me to abandon the system. I credit a book entitled *Time Power* (Hobbs, 1987) with showing me a very easy approach to documenting the events of the day. Finally, I had a system easy enough I would actually use it!

The standard Day-Timer or Franklin-Covey planner offers two facing pages for each day. The left-hand page houses appointments and tasks. The right-hand page provides a place for the type of documentation we will discuss. The same result can be accomplished with a loose-leaf binder and blank paper or a spiral notebook. If a legal pad or steno pad serves as the signature tool, the lower half of the page for that day can be used for documentation.

The page used for documentation will replace each of the following items:

- The notepad that lives by the phone.

- The back of the scrap envelope we reach for to jot a quick note.

- Post-Its stuck everywhere.

- The napkin in the purse left over from last night's dinner.

- The grocery list stuck to the refrigerator door.

In short, the documentation page provides a single place to capture anything we need to record during the course of the day. At the end of the day, decide what needs to be done about what was written.

Here are some examples of what one might find during a day's documentation:

- A friend calls extending an invitation to a party. While he is relaying the date, time, instructions on what to bring, and directions on how to get there, jot it all in one place—the documentation section of today's page. When the call is over, resume doing whatever it was you were doing, trusting that all of the information is safe.

- You place an order for some materials over the phone. While placing the order, jot on the documentation page the name of the salesperson, his/her extension, the order confirmation number, any discount promised, and other information that might be needed later.

♦ Saturday afternoon may happen to be the normal day for grocery shopping, so Saturday's documentation page is the place to make the grocery list. Every time you think of something you need, flip to Saturday, and jot it on that page.

♦ A parent has scheduled a conference for Thursday. Every time you think of something to discuss, open the signature tool to Thursday and enter it on the documentation page. You are building an agenda as you go. During the conference, take notes on the documentation page.

♦ At the end of the day, mentally review the day and identify significant events. Perhaps an award is bestowed on you or your school. An event has taken place which moves forward a school or personal goal. This page provides a place to capture those bits of good news. A shortened version of that good news can be inked on the month-at-a-glance calendar as an example of "How did you make today count?"

A quick review of that documentation page at the end of the day is vital in keeping the system alive. Look at what you have written throughout the day on today's documentation page and ask yourself, "What does this mean to me?" or "When will I need to see this again?"

The first example was an invitation to a party. When looking at those notes at the end of the day, they will be your cue to flip to the appropriate day in your signature tool and note the party in the appropriate time slot. You also see from your notes that there are a few items you are to bring. Flip to Saturday's page and jot on the task list a couple of items you need to buy at the grocery store.

On the day of the party, how are you going to remember what to bring? How are you going to remember how to get there? Here is the real magic of your documentation page—being able to go right back to information exactly when you need it.

Suppose the conversation about the party happened on May 10. As you review your notes at the end of the day, turn in your signature tool or month-at-a-glance calendar and write "Party" on the correct day and time slot. Put out beside it this notation—(5/10). Anything in parentheses in your signature tool tells you, *Go to this date for more information.* When it is time to leave for the party, that little note that says "(5/10)" tells you to look back in your signature tool to May 10. You are now looking at the notes you took on that date, and hence looking at a list of what to bring and directions on how to get there!

We have talked about taking notes on the documentation page when placing orders by phone. When the call is over, your documentation is over. At the end of the day, look at your notes and ask yourself what would be a reasonable amount of time to allow for the order to arrive. Flip ahead in your signature tool and in the to-do section, write "Acme (5/10)." When that date arrives, that entry sends you back in your signature tool to May 10, the day the order was placed with Acme. When calling to check on the order, the phone number with extension, the name of the person spoken with, the confirmation number, and all other needed information is at your fingertips.

This next scenario is a very common one—the teacher taking notes during a call from a parent and following through with the action required. You find in your mailbox one of those little pink slips of paper that says John Smith's father has called. You return the call and take some notes while on the phone. Do not write down everything that is said, but instead simply jot down the important points. If the date is October 25, you are going to be writing on documentation page for October 25. During the conversation, jot down the name. Beside the name, jot the phone number. Now, throw away that little pink slip of paper!

The father tells you about the problem. He says that other students are picking on his son during your class. While listening, you are probably formulating ideas on how you will handle the situation, perhaps talking individually with several students who sit in that area of the room to gain a perspective on what may be happening. You promise to look into the situation. You also tell the father that you will call him back in two weeks to see if there has been any recurrence of the problem. During the course of the conversation, Mr. Smith rambles a bit and tells you about the house in which the family will be moving and even tells you where it is located. While he talks, you continue to jot a few notes.

When the phone call is over, the documentation is over! There is nothing to recopy, nothing to file. Now, let us take a look at what you might have written in the signature tool as illustrated in Figure 4.2

Notice that during the conversation, you created two "to-do" items for yourself:

1. Talking with three boys who may be able to offer valuable information.

2. Call Mr. Smith back in two weeks.

The asterisk (*) is my symbol that what is written is not just information, but is something requiring action on my part.

Figure 4.2. Example of Documentation

> Oct. 25
>
> John Smith—362–1234
>
> Father called. Says other students are picking on son in Math class.
>
> * Speak with Sam, Tim, and Jerry about what they have noticed.
> * Call him back in 2 weeks to ask about progress.
>
> Are moving into new house this weekend. Directions: Head north on main street. Turn right on Maple. 3rd house on left.

You would probably jot a note in the lesson plan book or next day's to-do list to talk to the three boys. Here is how you to handle the second point, calling Mr. Smith two weeks later. Flip ahead two weeks in the signature tool and on the task list, write what is shown in Figure 4.3. You can now forget all about Mr. Smith. He is off your mind.

Figure 4.3. Task Referring Back to Documentation

Call Mr. Smith (10/25)

Two weeks later, when you look at your signature tool, "Call Mr. Smith" is in the task list. The notation "(10/25)" tells you to look at October 25. Anything in parentheses in the planner means "look here for more information." Flip back to October 25th and you are suddenly back to the notes made during that conversation. The name, the phone number, a summary of the conversation, and the commitments made during that conversation are all there.

While returning the call to Mr. Smith, you will be looking at the notes taken two weeks ago. Although you may not have given those notes or that conversation another moment's thought since the original conversation, you are able to demonstrate a good grasp of what had been discussed. You are also establishing a reputation with this man of being someone who can follow through on commitments.

During the conversation, you might also say, "By the way, how are things coming with the new house? Let me see if I remember what you had told me. If I go down Main Street and take a right on Maple, isn't it the third house on the left?" Mr. Smith will think you have a great memory! Maybe you do have a good memory. Maybe you just have a good system. Mr. Smith never needs to know the difference!

We have all experienced placing an order on the telephone and it not coming as expected. All too often, the conversation sounds something like this: "This is Penelope Jones and I talked to somebody there about ordering some stuff and it's been a long time and it still hasn't come."

Why did the conversation sound the way it did? Perhaps Penelope simply did not document at all during the phone call. Perhaps she took careful notes, but they were on the back of a scrap envelope that is now nowhere to be found.

What if Penelope had used the technique outlined in this chapter? During the call, she would have jotted down the name of the business and the phone number. She would have also written the name of the salesman and his extension number. When he gave her the order number, she would write that down as well. She would also make a note about the 15% discount he promised her. Finally, she records that the salesman has promised the order will arrive in ten business days.

When Penelope gets off the phone, she flips ahead two weeks on her signature tool and writes "Acme Inc." In parentheses, she writes today's date. Penelope may now close the planner and forget all about Acme. Two weeks later, she will see a reminder in her task list concerning this order. If the order has not arrived, Penelope will be on the telephone. This time, however, the conversation will be different:

> Could I speak to Sam Johnson at extension 718? Hi Sam, this is Penelope Jones. I am calling about order number 54321 which I placed on March 15th. You had said it would arrive within 10 business days. It has now been 15 business days and the material still has not come. Could you check on the status of that order for me? The amount will be how much? Sam, you specifically told me I would get a 15% discount. I wrote that down in my planner when we talked.

No one is going to argue when you are armed this type of information, and you are sure to get better service.

Monthly "Table of Contents"

When you want to find a particular piece of information in a book, how do you do it? Rather than thumb through every page, you are likely to go to the table of contents or the index. You are able to scan quickly for a mention of the needed topic and find a page number housing the more detailed information. We can use the same concept with our documentation.

In the example with Mr. Smith and with Penelope, we wrote information on the documentation page and knew exactly when we would need it again. What about the information that you may need again, but don't know when? For example, you order a printer and speak with a particularly helpful salesman. Six months later, you need to order another printer and wish you could put your hands on the notes from that conversation. As another example, you teach 150 students each day as a high school teacher. You hold a parent conference and jot notes on the documentation page. Six months later, you need to find your notes from that conference. How do you put your hands on them?

There is no need to thumb through all of those pages looking for that information. By constructing our own "table of contents," referring back to older information becomes easy. A little ritual that requires about twenty minutes at the end of each month will allow any piece of information to be found in seconds.

This table of contents could be composed on paper. Head the page with the name of the month and year. List the days of the month side of the page. Beside each number, write a key word or two about any piece of documentation for that day that could be of lasting value.

Better yet, the table of contents could be constructed electronically allowing for easy searching. One document will house the documentation not just for one month, but instead it will serve as a table of contents for years. Figure 4.4 (page 64) illustrates how one month's documentation would look. If a digital table of contents is your choice, do not create a different document for each month. Your electronic table of contents will house months and years worth of entries. One month follows the next down the page.

To add a new month to the table of contents, sit down at the computer with the planner and pull up your electronic document. Look at the documentation for the first day of the month, enter a "1" and add a key word or two for any item on that date that is of "lasting value." In our example, nothing of significance was documented for May 1 or 2. May 3 has three entries that might need to be referenced again. One involved a company called "Barber Sales." Another involving someone named "Dodd." A third involved Jane at a company called "BCI." Continue the process for each day in the month. Generally, the entire process can be completed in twenty minutes.

The beauty of the electronic table of contents is that we need not visually scan the page. Instead, use the "find" command built into Microsoft Word, or similar programs, to locate information. When looking for a particular piece of information, open the table of contents. Begin the "find" command with Ctrl+F. Enter a key word. The software will land on each occurrence of that term. Pressing Enter will move from one occurrence of that term to the next. In just a few seconds, you will find the piece of information you need.

Figure 4.4. Example of Monthly Table of Contents

May 2010

3. Barber Sale, Dodd, BCI Jane

4. Sue Smith top prize

5. Cookie dough salesman Jones, Milkbox repair

6. Montgomery IEP

7. Baker teacher complaint, Student Council field trip

11. Burns SYETP

12. Order printer MicroLowPrice

13. Pizza Hut compliment

14. Jones DHR attorney, Tate late, Donald Jones painter

17. Jeremy Davis conference retention

18. House paint

19. PowerPrint registered

20. XYA registration number

24. Sungate Records

27. Yearbook meeting

28. Copier lease

31. Manuscript mailed, ethics meeting

The following example illustrates how this procedure works. A teacher talks with a salesman at a particular company and orders a printer. During the conversation, the teacher writes the name of the company, the salesman, the phone number, order confirmation number, exactly what was being ordered, the price, any discount, and any other pertinent information. When the conversation ends, the teacher flips ahead a couple of weeks in the planner and makes an entry in the task list as a reminder to follow up if the order is not received as expected. Parentheses containing today's date will point the teacher back to all of the notes taken during the conversation. The order arrives on schedule, and the teacher checks off the task as "done."

Six months later, the teacher wants to order an additional printer and remembers how helpful that salesman had been and how reasonable the price had been. If only the teacher could find the notes the teacher had taken, the teacher could easily reach that same company and salesman! The electronic table of contents allows the teacher to do just that.

The teacher opens the document and enlists the help of the "find" command. What key term might be used? "Printer" comes to mind, so the teacher enters the word printer in the search window. The search lands on the term in the midst of the entry that says, "12. Order printer MicroLowPrice" (see Figure 4.4, page 64). This line was a part of the section labeled "May 2010." The teacher now pulls the documentation taken during May 2010 and flips to May 12. The notes taken during that conversation are now in front of the teacher. On the next attempt to contact the company, the telephone number for the company, the name and extension for the particular salesman, as well as all of the details from that conversation will be at hand.

Every day, we are involved in phone calls and conferences with parents. At the time of the conversation, we have little clue as to the need for any documentation. The conversation may simply be routine. On the other hand, what seemed like a routine conversation may erupt into a volatile situation several weeks later. You never know when you will need your documentation.

Because most of what is documented will never be accessed again, we do not want to spend a great deal of time in the documentation process. Take a few notes while you are on the phone or in conference. When the conversation is over, the documentation is over. Twenty minutes at the end of the month insures that you can put your hands on any of it whenever you need it. That is easy enough you might actually do it!

Future Tasks

Obviously, not every task you have set out for yourself is going to be accomplished during the coming week. We all need some place to trap the tasks that need to be done, yet we do not plan to get to them this week.

In the back of the planner, label a page "Future Tasks" and use that page to list any new task that comes your way that will not be completed this week. Depending on the number of tasks, several pages may be required. The first could be devoted to tasks for later this month, one for tasks to be accomplished the next month, and so forth.

Next Steps

♦ Look at your current to-do list or task list. After reading this chapter, do you see problems with your list? Can you rewrite the tasks in a way that makes them clearer and more doable?

♦ Before making a firm decision about what you will use as your signature tool, read Chapter 3. Give serious thought to which will better suit your needs: a paper system or a digital-based system.

♦ If your decision is paper, make a trip to your local office supply store and look at the selection of planners available for purchase. Remember, the major functions your tool must handle are calendar items, tasks, and documentation. Also remember that your signature tool is one that will be with you everywhere you go.

♦ If your choice for a signature tool is paper, go ahead and establish a monthly table of contents on your computer now, even before you have anything to enter into it. Merely establishing it is the first step towards adding to it each month.

♦ Enter a task for the last day of this month reminding you to update your electronic table of contents. Do the same for the next couple of months. After reading Chapter 5, you may want the *repeating task system* you establish to handle this reminder for you.

5

Think It Through Once: Handling Repeating Tasks

We are what we repeatedly do. Excellence, therefore, is not an act, but a habit.

— Aristotle

Education is a Cyclic Business

The start of each new school year brings dreams for the months ahead. We will be initiating new projects and trying new ideas. We will also be repeating some of last year's projects. What tasks do we need to perform so we will be *ready* when students walk through the door? What materials will we need? What orientation activities will we have for new students?

As we think through the year and the projects we will undertake, other thoughts occur. What plans need to be made to successfully complete each project? Do we need to reserve buses? What information will we prepare and send to parents? What purchase orders will be needed?

The old saying "the devil is in the details" is certainly true in education. Let one of the myriad of details slip though the cracks and you are faced with a group of students ready for the field trip—and no bus. Not only that, but there are no sack lunches prepared for the students because you forgot to speak to the lunchroom manager about preparing them. The check you will need to present at your destination almost didn't get written because you forgot to request it until yesterday afternoon.

The good news for those of us in the business of education is that many of the same "devils" return every year and at the same time. The first time a big project, such as starting a school year or planning the trip to Washington is undertaken, little "to-dos" will occur to you at the most unlikely of moments—in the middle of a meeting, during lunch, or while pushing the shopping cart down the aisle of the grocery store. When they occur, the habit of trapping them with the signature tool will keep a good idea or essential detail from disappearing.

There is even better news. Once a project has been handled once, you should never have to rethink *any* of those details. Never again will you sit with a blank legal pad two weeks before the start of school trying to pull a list out of your head of what you need to be doing. Never again will you rethink all of the details that went into the big "spring production." The truth of the matter is all of the details needed to be handled *this* year are the same ones handled *last* year, if you only had a system to keep track of them.

This chapter provides a system for identifying and capturing all of the repeating tasks that come your way. Without such a plan, you are in for a frustrating experience as you "reinvent the wheel" year after year.

Setting Up a Repeating Task System

Life gets easier when a system handles all of the details that recur each year, month, week, or even each day. The first step in establishing this tool is to become very good at *recognizing repeating tasks as soon as they appear*. Consider these two items:

1. Call Mrs. Smith

2. Order blank certificates for Awards Day

Each represents a simple phone call. Each can be handled in just a few minutes. The two, however, are vastly different. Once the call to Mrs. Smth is completed, the task is checked off and nothing more needs to be done. On the other hand, ordering the certificates for the annual Awards Day ceremony is a task that will repeat every year. Forget that one phone call, let that one detail slip through the cracks, and the sponsor of this event will be looking at quite a problem when there are no certificates on hand to present at the ceremony.

Getting very good at recognizing repeating tasks when they first present themselves is *crucial* in keeping things from falling through the cracks. When you find yourself writing a task which will repeat at regular intervals, take the time to put it into your *repeating task system*. This practice saves time and effort when those tasks return a week, a month, or a year later. What does a repeating task system look like? Here are three alternatives.

Repeating Tasks on Index Cards

Index cards, used in conjunction with tickler files, offer a low-tech method for insuring repeating tasks are completed according to schedule without having to give them another thought. Each time you identify a repeating task, take an index card and write the task in the middle of the card. Toward the bottom of the card, write instructions on how the card should be refiled once the task has been completed.

During the middle of the summer, you decide it would be a nice idea to send a letter to your new students welcoming them to your class. You realize the job would be much easier if you have a set of mailing labels for the envelopes, saving time over having to handwrite the name and address of every student. So, you add to your task list a reminder to see the school's administrative assistant about getting a set of mailing labels. After receiving the labels, you would check it off. That sounds like what this book has been suggesting. Right?

The problem with this approach is there is no trigger to remind you to see the secretary about mailing labels *a year from now*. Instead, you must realize this task is something that will occur not one time, but instead returns every summer. Using the index card system, you would pull a blank card and notate on it something like what you see in Figure 5.1.

Figure 5.1. Using Index Cards for Repeating Tasks

> See administrative assistant to get
> address labels for incoming students.
>
> *Refile for July 10 of next year*

Once the instructions have been written on the card, you will never again have to "remember" to get those mailing labels again. After obtaining the labels, drop the card in the tickler file for July and forget about it. Next July, the card reappears. Perform the task again and refile the card.

After truly identifying all of the routine tasks performed during the course of the year, do not be surprised if the number runs into several hundred. With the index card system, these routine tasks pop up at just the right time. The important point is that the system does the remembering, and you are now free to move on to more creative thought.

Repeating Task List

An advantage of the index card is its simplicity. The disadvantage is the inability to see *all* of the repeating tasks at one time. One cannot see a total picture of just how many of them exist, how heavy or light any particular time of the year may be, or which tasks must be handled personally versus which can be delegated.

A second option exists for those using a paper signature tool. This option involves putting the repeating tasks together on one chronological list. To establish this list, the following procedure will prove helpful:

1. Every time a task is added in your signature tool, pay special attention to whether it will be performed at routine intervals. Put a *red star,* beside any such task.

2. Perform the task and check it off. The number of red stars will naturally increase over the course of the next few months.

3. During the winter holidays, compile a Repeating Task List. Collect the pages from your signature tool for the last several months. Use them to create a new document entitled *Repeating Task List*.

4. Carefully examine all of the past pages from the signature tool looking for red stars. Enter each starred item onto your list. Group the tasks chronologically by month.

5. During the summer, compile the same type of list with the red-starred items collected between the winter break and present. Print the list, put a staple in one corner, and the entire year's inventory of repeating tasks in at your fingertips.

6. Keep the *Repeating Task List* in your tickler file. Each time it pops up, perform the task and then re-file the entire list for next date it will be needed.

The *Repeating Task List* is an idea that will work regardless of the particular position a person holds. The nature of the tasks on the list will differ depending on whether one is a classroom teacher, building-level administrator, or central office administrator. The basic idea, however, remains the same.

The *Repeating Task List* is ideal for handling those responsibilities that arise no more frequently than once per month. For weekly or daily repeating tasks, using the index cards process is the better solution.

Figure 5.2 shows a few sample tasks from a teacher's repeating list for July. None of the tasks is particularly hard to perform, yet even the simplest one allowed to slip through the cracks will cause problems later. Every teacher has repeating tasks that are unique to the specific school or situation.

You must develop the ability to recognize a repeating task immediately and be able to put it in the system.

Figure 5.2. Sample Repeating Task List

Update forms for this month from monthly tickler on computer

Compile order for office supplies

Plan small holiday gifts for students (Halloween, Christmas, Valentine's Day)

Backup computer

Decide what field trips the class will take

Put all dates from school master calendar on personal calendar

Update welcome letter to students

Secure address labels for welcome letters

Put up bulletin board

Inventory textbooks

Repeating Tasks in Outlook

Repeating tasks are a breeze for those who organize digitally. Each time a repeating task arises, click the "recurrence" button, and define how often the task should show up on the list. Figure 5.3 (page 72) shows where repeating patterns would be established on Outlook. Handheld devices will have a similar option.

Keeping Your Sanity with Repeating Tasks

Visit the classroom of any teacher, and you are likely to see a shelf or more of manuals, each filled with tasks to be performed. Those manuals may include some of the following:

♦ *Teacher Evaluation Manual*—This manual, perhaps over four inches thick, is laden with timelines and procedural land mines for both the teacher and the administrator.

Figure 5.3. Repeating Tasks in Outlook

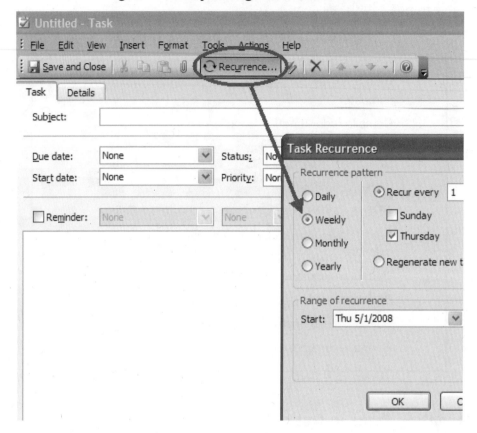

◆ *Crisis Plan*—Nobody doubts the importance of keeping students safe. A thick manual, however, is neither easily accessible nor practical in a real crisis and does not necessarily ensure a safe school.

◆ *State Law*—One's state may produce a volume containing the laws governing education. Many procedures must be carried out annually because of requirements found in that book.

◆ *Board of Education Policy*—Embedded are tasks that must be performed at various points in the year. Trying to commit each of them to memory and hoping one thinks to perform them at the right time is asking for trouble.

◆ *Course of Study*—With all of the manuals on the shelf, let us not forget the reason schools exist is to teach students. The Course of Study for each discipline outlines content, requirements for graduation, and time requirements.

Each manual is written in isolation. No one ties them together for the teacher. No one combs through the collection and then hands the teacher a comprehensive list of what need to be done during the month of *August* to satisfy the requirements of all of the various sources. No one puts it all together in one big "ball of wax." That job is for the *teacher*. A similar scenario exists for the superintendent, curriculum director, principal, assistant principal, department head, or anyone else in the school system.

The good news is there is a way to preserve some sanity, and the *Repeating Task System* is it. While reading through any one of those manuals, tasks that must be performed routinely will leap off the page. At that point, put them in the system. Jot them on index cards for the tickler files, add them to the repeating list, or enter them as repeating tasks in Outlook. Now, forget about them and trust that your system will bring each one to your attention at the right time. Your *Repeating Task System* is the glue, the "whole ball of wax" that puts all of the tasks in one place and makes them "get in line."

Next Steps

- ◆ Decide how you will structure your repeating tasks. Will you use index cards dropped in tickler files, a list composed and saved on the computer, or repeating tasks on a digital tool?

- ◆ Schedule a block of time to think through the projects you handle each year. List all of the tasks associated with each one. Review the list several times to see if additional tasks come to mind.

- ◆ Schedule another block of time during the winter holiday break to review the repeating tasks for the remainder of the year. Additional tasks may come to mind that were not evident during the original planning session.

- ◆ Decide if the idea of the Repeating Task System is something you would like to expand throughout the school. Consider discussing your system with fellow teachers or your administrators to see if it is something they might wish to implement.

6

Handling Multiple Projects

The secret of getting ahead is getting started. The secret of getting started is breaking your complex and overwhelming tasks into small manageable tasks and then starting on the first one.

— Mark Twain

Our proudest accomplishments and our more disheartening frustrations are often associated with goals we have set and ambitious projects we have undertaken. None were accomplished with one simple act. Instead, over a period of time, one task after another was performed, plans were adjusted and readjusted, follow up and follow through were demonstrated, and problems were solved as glitches arose. The end result was a "job well done."

On the other hand, we all can name a few endeavors we would like to forget. The job kept bogging down. We were never quite sure what had been done and what needed to be done next. The whole thing was a big, ugly fog that finally died a natural death, to which we exclaimed, "Good riddance."

What Makes Projects Different?

Projects are entirely different from other tasks on the list. Checking off a single task does not complete a project or realize a goal. We achieve goals and accomplish projects through *multiple steps*. Sometimes, we can list every step in the project from beginning to end. With others, the steps unfold as we work. To compound the problem, teachers are generally handling multiple projects at any one time. How in the world can we keep it all straight?

The following example illustrates how complex even a relatively simple project can become. Imagine a teacher who wants to acquire a digital whiteboard for the classroom. The goal obviously would be accomplished when the teacher sees the board installed on the wall.

The teacher believes the first step toward accomplishing the goal is to talk to the principal. In other schools, an assistant principal or technology coordinator might be the correct person. In any case, the next step for the teacher is to schedule a time to talk to that one person about the possibility of getting a digital whiteboard. What about the second step? As the next paragraph illustrates, that answer is not so clear.

During that meeting, the decision maker may state that several digital whiteboards are already on order, that the administration has been trying to decide who will get them, and that the teacher's request will be granted. At that point, the teacher's next step would simply be to follow up with the administrator about installation.

On the other hand, the teacher could be told that funds were tight and perhaps the PTA could help with the purchase of a board. In this case, the teacher's next step would be to fill out the proper form and write a short proposal to go with it in order to submit it to the PTA.

A third scenario might be an upfront assurance that not only is there no money in the budget, but that PTA coffers are dry as well. At this point, the teacher might think in terms of anything from requesting funds from a legislator to hosting a bake sale.

The outcome of that *one conversation* with the administrator could lead to *three* entirely different second steps. Each of those three responses would send the project in a different direction, and that is after only a single step! Imagine how many different twists and turns could take place over the life of the project. A timeline for securing all of the needed funds, choosing a vendor, and negotiating a deal are among the steps between here and that digital whiteboard being used with students.

Projects often work just that way. Keep in mind this is but one project. The same teacher may have several dozen projects going on at the same time, each of them ranging in various degrees of complexity and various degrees of completion.

Keeping projects on track involves some very specific strategies, which are described throughout this chapter:

- ◆ Define the goal.

- ◆ Break the project into small steps.

- ◆ Feed projects into the task list.

- Keep related notes with the project.
- Stick with a project as long as you can.
- Put a "bookmark" in the project.
- Handle supporting material.
- Link the tickler files to the task list.

Define the Goal

Handling a project begins with defining the goal. What will the project look like when complete? How will you know when you have achieved your goal? Taking the time to state your goals clearly saves a great deal of time implementing them. Figure 6.1 is an example of projects the teacher may be addressing:

Figure 6.1. Example of Defined Goals

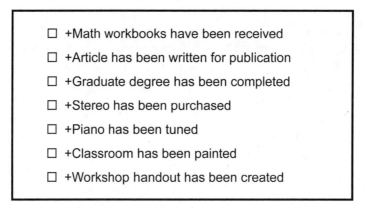

- ☐ +Math workbooks have been received
- ☐ +Article has been written for publication
- ☐ +Graduate degree has been completed
- ☐ +Stereo has been purchased
- ☐ +Piano has been tuned
- ☐ +Classroom has been painted
- ☐ +Workshop handout has been created

Phrase the goal as a statement written in the past tense. Word it as if it has already been achieved. Place a noun toward the beginning of the statement. Each statement is either *true* or *false*. Once that statement is *true*, the project can be checked off as "done." As long as the statement is *false*, more work is ahead.

Your signature tool is the place to record the goal. Exactly where should it be recorded? The answer depends on the tool. Using a paper system, include pages in the back of the planner. Label the goal at the top of the page and number it. In the space available, write all of the steps that occur to you as well as any related information that comes your way. Figure 6.2 (page 77) is an example of a project planning page.

Figure 6.2. Project Planning Page

#1 Calendar for new school year has been adopted

    1. Establish initial meeting

    2. Send out invitations for initial meeting

    3. Establish agenda for initial meeting

    4. Publicize two calendars for votes

    5. Establish meeting to tally votes

    6. Establish dates for kindergarten registration, reporting period dates, and report cards dates.

    7. Make recommendation to superintendent

    8. Publicize new calendars to schools

Topics to discuss:

    1. Spring break after testing?

    2. Concentrate professional development days at beginning of year or space throughout the year?

    3. Fall break or not?

    4. Equal days first and second semester

If the signature tool is digital, enter the goal in the *task list*. Notice in Figure 6.1 (page 76), that each goal begins with a + sign. That symbol sets a goal apart from the single tasks on the list. The + sign sitting at the beginning of the line serves as an alert that an important element is missing. We discuss that omission in the next section.

Break the Project into Small Steps

With some projects, it is possible to define all of the steps from the beginning to end. With others, it may be possible to define only the very next step. As with the example of securing a digital whiteboard, the teacher could only define the first step.

For those who use a paper system, list on that planning page all of the steps you know, just as shown in Figure 6.2. For those using a digital tool, the place to list this information is in a note attached to the task. Figure 6.3 shows a sample project planned in Outlook. Figure 6.4 provides an example on a handheld device.

Figure 6.3. Project Planning in Outlook

Subject:	+Teacher of the Year/JSU Hall of Fame have been submitted and winners honored				
Start date:	Tue 12/1/2009	Status:	Not Started		
Due date:	Tue 12/1/2009	Priority:	Normal	% Complete:	0%
☐ Reminder:	None	None	🔊 Owner:	Dr. Frank Buck	

+Teacher of the Year/JSU Hall of Fame have been submitted and winners honored
Look for electronic application. Last year's is at ftp://ftp.alsde.edu/documents/55/2009_2010_TOY_Application.pdf
Go here to look for new one: http://www.alsde.edu/html/sections/awards.asp?section=55&footer=sections

Set deadlines for submission of Teach of the Year and JSU Teacher Hall of Fame
Invite Members of District-Level Teacher of the Year Committee/JSU Committees
      Superintendent
      Board Member
      Parent Organization Representative
      Elementary Teacher
      Secondary Teacher
Duplicate applications
Collect applications
Score applications
Mail winning applications
Plan announcement of winners
Throw away all Teacher of the Year and JSU Hall of Fame application materials (Bulk).

Contact is Sharon Parks, (334) 555-9700 or astarks@alsde.edu

Figure 6.4. Project Planning on a Handheld Device

Title: Student Support Team

☐ Schedule SST refresher as part of beginning of school faculty meeting

☐ Compose schedule for SST meetings

☐ Examine tracking log to be sure it is up to date (monthly)

☐ Examine tracking log thoroughly

☐ Change outcome of anyone in the process to "Pending"

Feed Projects into the Task List

Paper Signature Tool

With a paper-based signature tool, you must somehow link the planning sheet in the back of the planner to the task list from which you are working.

To do this, take the first step from one of the goals and enter it into the task list. Beside the task, list the goal number in parentheses. This action creates a link between the task in the list and the goal. In Figure 6.5, the notation "(G1)" denotes this task is from Goal #1.

Figure 6.5. Task Linked Backed to Its Project

Harry—Send me copy of your proposed calendar (G1)

When the task is completed, that notation "(G1)" becomes important. Before checking the task off as "done," go to the back of the planner and pick up the next task listed for that goal. Every time one step toward achieving the goal is completed, the next step must be added to the task list. Otherwise, the project falls through the cracks.

Digital Signature Tool

If the signature tool is digital, feeding goals into the task list is even easier. Notice that Figure 6.1 (page 76) listed a series of goals. In each case, the line began with a + sign and to the right was the goal. For each goal, take the next step toward achieving that goal and place it to the left of the + sign. Figure 6.6 shows tasks and goals together. Working through the task list, the user can see not only *what* to do (the task), but *why* it is being done (the goal).

Figure 6.6. Tasks and Goals Together

When you complete a task, do not click the checkbox. Instead, replace the task just completed with the next step towards completing the project or achieving the goal. Figure 6.7 shows a project in Outlook. In this illustration, the teacher is in charge of the "Student Support Team" for the school. The first task is to schedule a refresher for the faculty. When this task is completed, cut the task and replace it with the next step—scheduling a series of meetings.

Figure 6.7. Replacing a Completed Task with the Next Task

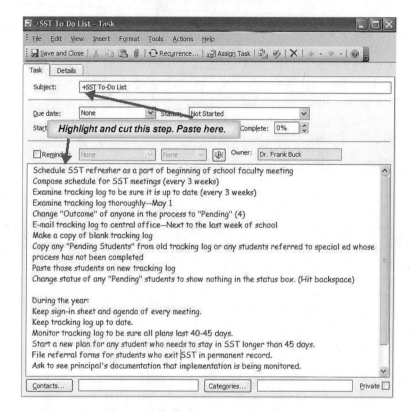

Keep Related Notes with the Project

During the life of any project, information will be generated about it. If the goal is to acquire a digital whiteboard, a list of various models and prices along with contact information for vendors will be developed at some point. Phone calls will be made and notes taken during those calls. Information will be generated from e-mails and website pages. If all of the information related to a project is kept together, finding that information becomes easy.

Paper Signature Tool

If you are using a paper tool, the planning sheet at the back is the place to keep notes from phone calls and any other information related to the project. Figure 6.2 (page 77) provides an illustration.

Digital Signature Tool

If you are using a digital signature tool, all information related to the project goes in the note section of the task. Figure 6.8 shows a goal, the next step toward achieving it, a list of steps to follow, notes from a phone call, and Internet links to related information. When synchronized with the handheld, the teacher has all of this information literally in the palm of the hand.

Figure 6.8. Information in Note Section of Task

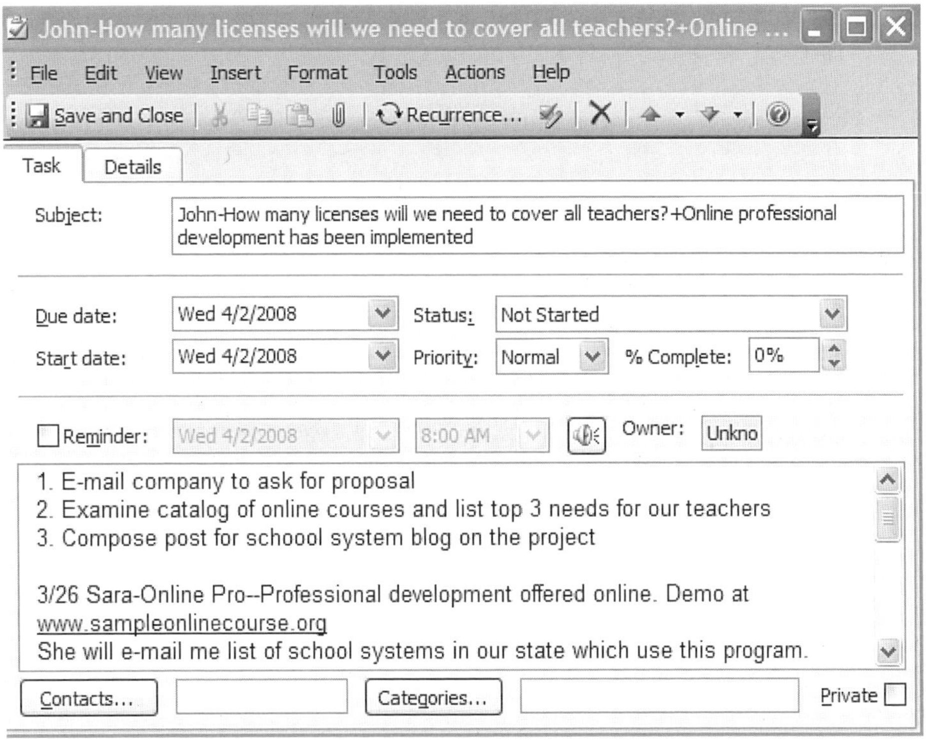

Stick with a Project as Long as You Can

One look at the task list reveals multiple projects represented. Should you perform the next step for "Goal 1," move to the next step for "Goal 2," and then handle the next step for "Goal 3"? Or should you stay with one project and work toward one goal?

More will be accomplished in the long run by sticking with one project as long as possible. One always experiences some time spent in "startup" when transitioning to a project. Gathering materials and getting mentally reacquainted with the project accompany each session. The more jumping back and forth from one project to the next, the more time will be spent with these transition activities.

Suppose you wanted to work on the "Student Support Team" project, a scenario examined earlier. The first step is to schedule time on a faculty meeting for a "refresher." Once that date is established, the teacher might be able to go right ahead and schedule dates for the meeting throughout the year. That would be as far as the teacher could take that project at that moment. The next step after scheduling meeting dates, the one regarding examining the tracking log, would be cut and pasted in the subject line. A new start and due date would be chosen so that task comes back at the right time.

Toward the end the year, the teacher comes upon a number of tasks relating to finalizing the tracking log, submitting it, and preparing for the next year. The teacher would be able to go from one step to the next, accomplishing all of these at one sitting:

♦ Change "Outcome" of anyone in the process to "Pending."

♦ E-mail tracking log to central office—next to the last week of school.

♦ Make a copy of blank tracking log.

♦ Copy any "Pending Students" from old tracking log or any students referred to special ed. whose process has not been completed.

♦ Paste those students on new tracking log.

♦ Change status of any "Pending" students to show nothing in the status box.

At some point, you would cease working on that project. Any number of reasons could account for needing to move on to something else:

♦ You have an appointment and need to move on to it.

♦ You have other urgent matters that need your attention and cannot afford to spend any more time on this project at this time.

♦ You are getting tired and need a break from the project.

♦ You need information that you do not have at hand in order to continue the project.

♦ You see that the next step towards accomplishing your goal is to contact another person, and that person is not available.

♦ You are interrupted by an emergency.

The list could go on. Whatever the reason for putting the project aside, you need a "bookmark."

Put a "Bookmark" in the Project

At one time or another each of us has read a book from cover to cover in one sitting. This experience, however, is the exception rather than the rule. For one reason or another, the book must be put aside to do something else. Just before closing the book, we *insert a bookmark*. This little tool tells exactly *where to begin* the next time we resume reading the book. The same type of reminder is needed when working on our projects.

We may work through step after step on a project. Just before we put the project aside, we must decide where to start next time. That task must go on our list before leaving the project.

Handle Supporting Material

Managing a project includes organizing and being able to access quickly the supporting material. For example, if the project is to write a grant, you will have the *Request for Proposal*, data others have supplied to you, letters of support, and pages of notes created. If the project is to set up a wireless computer network at home, you may have several articles clipped from magazines. If the project is to revise your school's writing program, you will likely have collected sample plans from other schools, articles from journals, and notes taken from workshops. Where do you keep all of this information? How do you link these items back to the project in your signature tool? The answer lies in a creative use of the tickler files.

First, here is how *not* use the tickler files.

♦ *Do not* select a date to work on the grant and put the papers related to it in the folder for that date.

♦ *Do not* pick a date to work on the wireless network and file the supporting material for that date.

♦ *Do not* pick a date to work on the writing program and file the supporting material for that date.

At first glance, you may wonder what is wrong with such an approach. After all, that seems to be exactly what you learned in Chapter 2. The problem is that a group of papers does not tell you *what* to do. At best, a collection of papers related to the grant would serve as a reminder to do *something* about that grant. Your task list (and project planning sheet, if planning with paper) is where you will define exactly what to do next on the project and what steps will follow from there. The supporting material does not drive the action. Instead, this material simply needs to be accessible when you need it.

In Chapter 2, we labeled hanging files 1 to 31 to make items go away and then come back on specific dates. We will now give the first twenty-six of those files a letter designation (1A, 2B, 3C,...26Z) and learn how to use the *letters*.

Link the Tickler Files to the Task List

As soon as the grant proposal crossed the desk, follow these steps to get the paper off of the desk yet easily retrievable, the tasks defined on the list, and achieve a clear head:

1. Scan the proposal quickly to determine what it is and if you wish to apply. For the sake of this example, suppose the grant is called "Reading for the Next Century."

2. Assuming you plan to apply, create a new task in Outlook and label the subject line "+Reading for the Next Century Grant has been submitted."

3. In the note section, enter important information gleaned from a quick glance at the proposal. Such information would include the due date, the grant award amount, and a one-sentence description of the grant. Of course, during the writing of the grant, you will think of many more tasks associated with the project. Valuable information will come your way, such as the name of someone else who was successful in writing a proposal for this grant in the past. All of this information will be entered in the note section of this one task.

4. You have supporting material in paper form. Go back to the subject line and add in parentheses "(R)". As with anything else in this system, a set of parentheses means "look here for additional information." The subject line now reads, "+Reading for the Next Century Grant has been submitted (R)."

5. Grab a blank manila file folder and label it "Reading for the Next Century Grant (R)."

6. Open the tickler file drawer and place the file folder in the "18R" folder and close the drawer.

7. Return to Outlook and ask the question, "What is the first step toward completing this project?"

8. Once you determine the first step, enter it to the left of the "+".

9. Choose an appropriate start and due date and save the task.

Now go on to anything else. The first step in completing this project has been defined and is in the task list. If you think of ideas related to this project, go back to Outlook, double-click on the project, and add the new ideas in the note section. If the paperwork associated with the project is needed, simply thinking about the name of the grant reveals where to go in the tickler files to find it. Figure 6.9 (page 85) is a screen shot of how the project will look.

The same concept is used for any papers that require action, yet have no date associated. This next example uses a paper planner as the signature tool. Suppose you are reading a magazine article about setting up a wireless network at home and contemplate doing the same thing. Follow these steps:

1. Clip the article.

2. Take two seconds to determine what key word would be associated with this article. Perhaps the first thought is "wireless."

Figure 6.9. Project Involving a Reading Grant

Task	Details

Subject: +Reading for the Next Century Grant has been submitted (R)

| Due date: | Thu 7/10/2008 | Status: | Not Started |
| Start date: | Sun 6/1/2008 | Priority: | Normal | % Complete: | 0% |

☑ Reminder: Thu 7/10/2008 | 8:00 AM | Owner: |

Due August 1
$30,000
Purpose is to raise reading achievement among students from high-poverty background

Previous winners--Jefferson Elementary (www.jeffelem.org); Coker School www.cokerschool.com)

3. Flip to the back of the planner to a blank page and write on the top line: "Wireless network has been set up at home. (W)"

4. On the article, put "(W)" in the upper right hand corner.

5. Open the tickler file drawer and put the article in the "23W" file.

6. Decide what the first step toward completing this project is going to be. Perhaps you are going to ask a colleague (John in this example) for his recommendations. In the planner, this task would look like Figure 6.10.

Figure 6.10. Wireless Home Network Project

Wireless network has been set up at home. (W)

   1. John—What are your recommendations?

   2. Google—Wireless network purchasing.

   3. Call Computer World 555–8181. Ask about upcoming sales.

Whether the subject is the reading grant, the wireless network, or any project, the signature tool manages the flow of the project. If supporting material exists, the use of parentheses at the end of the task line points to that supporting material. If someone wants to see the paperwork on the "Reading for the Next Century Grant," think in terms of the key word "reading" and immediately pull the material from the "R" folder.

The Daily Drill

Upon arrival in the classroom, opening Outlook and pulling the tickler file for the day are the first two orders of business. In the tickler folder, you will see two types of items:

1. Items related to that *date*. At some time in the past, you had decided these papers needed to come back to your attention on this particular day, such as the birthday card that needs to go in the mail today, the agenda for today's board of education meeting, or the tickets to tonight's concert. These papers will be removed from the tickler file and handled.

2. Items related to that *letter*. Examples would include the manila file with the grant materials or the wireless network article. Leave these items in the folder and place this file at the back of the rack, where it will resurface a month from now.

How will you tell quickly which items are date specific and which constitute supporting material for items on the task list? If an item is supporting material, in the upper right corner, you should have a *letter in parentheses*. The wireless network article, for example, will have a "(W)" in the upper right corner.

After the Dance: What to Do When a Project is Complete

You now have a system for staying on top of multiple projects and seeing them to their completion. When the project is "done," when the goal has been achieved, what happens to the planning page in the back of your paper signature tool or the task in your digital tool? What happens to the file of supporting material?

Consider whether or not you need a "paper trail." Perhaps this same project or a similar one will be undertaken in the future. Perhaps the notes from this project will be shared with someone else. Depending on the project, the requirement that records be maintained for a certain period of time is highly probable. If you see no reason to keep any of the material, put the supporting paperwork in the trash can. Use a paper shredder for anything which could possibly be confidential. If you are not required to keep it, and you see no value in keeping it, get rid of it.

The same is true of the planning sheet from the back of your paper signature tool. If it has no value, throw it away or shred it. For those with a digital signature tool, simply check the task off as "done."

If you save records from your project, spending just a little time with cleanup makes the difference between concise records that are self-explanatory years later and the burden of picking up a thick folder barely decipherable. Go through the supporting folder item by item. Get rid of duplicate copies and cryptic notes. If your signature tool is paper, the planning sheet can also go in this same folder. If organizing digitally, you may wish to print the task containing all of your notes and put it in this folder as well. Although I am not a fan of printing digital reference material, the benefits of keeping everything in one place outweigh the downside of creating more paper.

When the paperwork is neatly organized, label a single file folder, and let the completed project join the reference files. If someone needs to review the project, the information in the folder can be found quickly.

Building a Reputation for "Staying on Top of Things"

You can stay on top of multiple projects. At times, you may feel like a juggler. In a way, your role in handling multiple projects and the role of a juggler are much the same. A juggler keeps a number of balls in the air by *giving each one a little attention on a regular basis*. The juggler knows just how many objects he has in the air, where each one is, when attention is needed, and how much attention is needed. We need to know exactly the same thing about each of our projects.

Certainly, none of us should take on more than we can handle well. For each of us, a limit does exist. The reality of teaching is that we have much on our plates. We need tools to help us stay on top of it all. This chapter gives you those tools. You can not only handle multiple projects, but you can make it look easy.

Next Steps

♦ Schedule a time to make a list of the projects that are currently in progress or are planned for the future. Do not try to fill in details at this point.

♦ Once you have identified all of the projects, enter each one in your signature tool. If that tool is paper, complete a planning page in the back of the planner for each project. If that tool is digital, create a new task for each, start the line with a + and define your goal.

♦ Begin with the projects already in progress. List as many steps in the project as possible. For those using a digital signature tool, list the steps in the note section of each task.

♦ Pull together information about the projects that are on scraps of paper or in your memory. Enter all of that information with its project.

♦ Identify the next step in each project and enter each one in your task list.

♦ For those projects you will not begin until sometime in the future, do not worry about identifying the first step in the project. For digital tools, the + sign with nothing to the left of it will identify that project as one not currently in progress.

7

Organizing Your Students

Perhaps the most valuable result of all education is the ability to make yourself do the thing you have to do, when it ought to be done, whether you like it or not; it is the first lesson that ought to be learned; and however early a man's training begins, it is probably the last lesson that he learns thoroughly.

— Thomas Henry Huxley, English biologist (1825–1895)

Experienced teachers have learned that school success and intelligence do not always go hand-in-hand. Often, very bright young people fail to turn in assignments, lose their work, and spend inordinate amounts of time frantically looking for things on a messy desk.

At the same time, other students breeze through school. They seem to make school look easy, but not because they are necessarily smarter than their peers. They have acquired some very easy, very teachable habits.

Organization is a gift that wise teachers give their students, and it is a gift that is useful long after the goodbyes are said in May. Ultimately, it is a gift that gives back in terms of reducing stress level for both the teacher and the students. More time is spent on what truly matters—teaching and learning. Less time is spent on the frustration of forgotten responsibilities and giving numerous reminders. This chapter examines the critical elements that experience has shown make a world of difference.

The Student Planner—
The Student's Signature Tool

Habits that help adults often also help students. The reverse of that point is also true. Good habits developed during one's youth pay lifelong dividends. Because the most basic organizational habit for adults is to write things down as soon as the thought occurs, then writing things down is also paramount for students. If writing the thought down is important, having a place to write it must also be important. Two chapters in this book have introduced the teacher to the *signature tool*. To think that only adults need this type of structure is a mistake. Young people today have many activities on which they must focus their attention—homework, athletic practices, family activities, and chores represent just some of their obligations. For them, just as with adults, the easy thing to do is let pencil and paper do the remembering. Get it on paper and you can get it off your mind! A student planner is the perfect tool for this purpose. It traps all commitments in one place.

Some students will come to this conclusion themselves. Many will resort to writing assignments on scraps of papers which are invariably lost. Others will simply try to remember it all. It is the teacher who will model and reinforce good organizational habits just as he or she does with any academic subject.

Selecting a Planner

For student planners to be used, teachers and students must see those little books as *making things easier*. Uniformity is one key consideration. If several different page layouts are represented amongst class members, that small point may cause just enough confusion to resist consistent use of the planner. Rather than leaving the purchase of the planner to each individual parent, look for sources that will allow you to purchase the same style for every student and issue them at the beginning of the year.

As a principal, I had success writing small grants to fund this type of purchase. The school PTA/PTO could likely see this project as worthy to fund for a class or for the entire school. After all, we are in the business of preparing young people to be successful at every stage in their lives. Helping students organize their lives and manage their time is an extremely worthy endeavor.

Planners generally come in two formats. One displays each week on two facing pages with each day being listed one below the other. The second displays the days on the week and subjects in a grid, very similar to a teacher's lesson plan book. In most cases, the second option is the more logical. The student is able to look in one direction and see the plan for the day or look in the other direction and see the plan for the entire week in any one subject.

The planner should not be used just for school assignments. It can and should be the one place which traps every responsibility. As students list athletic games and practices, after-school activities, school projects, as well as day-to-day assignments, they begin to see the *big picture* and can begin to budget their time. Therefore, it is important for the planner to have a place for students to list their outside-of-school commitments as well.

Students Planners in the Daily Routine

The complaint, "My students don't use their planners" is not a new one. If you pass out planners and mention nothing much more about them, you should not be surprised if students do not use them. Like many other lessons in life, you will first guide them fairly explicitly in the formation of good habits.

Students should be writing in their planners every day and in every class. Getting students to use the planner has as much to do with the terminology the teachers uses as anything else. I encourage you to banish from your vocabulary the phrase, "Now, don't forget to...." After all, do we really think that *telling* someone not to forget is actually going to prevent forgetting from happening? Instead of telling students *not* to forget, we should be telling them what *to* do. Replace "don't forget" with the words "open your planners."

Tell your students *what* to write and *where* to write it. After a while, they grasp the idea and need less direction. As an elementary school principal, Monday morning's announcements invariably included the instructions, "Open your planners to this week's page." Over the intercom, I went over the events coming up for the week and told the students what to write. If school pictures were to made on Friday, my words would be something like, "On Friday's square, write *Pictures*. When you see this, it will remind you that we will be taking pictures for the yearbook so that you will choose something nice to wear that day."

When teachers guide students through what to write and where to write it, they model the behaviors that students will later internalize. Some teachers may partition a section of their whiteboard where they list what students are to write each day. Others may even have a large-size replica of the student planner pages either on posters attached to the wall or saved as digital files and projected onto the screen.

What Do I Write and Where?

Think back in this book to the discussion of the signature tool and the importance of documentation. The well-structured system has a place to trap the raw communication as it arrives. Later in the day, we make decisions concerning what we need to do about the things we wrote. The results of those decisions show up as entries on our calendars or tasks scheduled for specific days.

Trapping the communication and *dissecting* it are two entirely different functions. Sometimes the communication is simple enough that we can simply make an entry on our calendar or to-do list. If Mary asks if you can have lunch on Saturday, a quick glance at the calendar shows if time is free. You enter the time and location straight on the calendar and nothing else needs to be done. On the other hand, what if that lunch invitation required calling to make a reservation and you are the one going to handle that task? What if transportation needs to be arranged for you or Mary? The more details involved, the more difficult it is to think of everything on the fly and record it all in the correct places. What is needed is the ability to jot, "Plan lunch on Saturday with Mary," go on with life, and then revisit that note at a time when you can think through the details.

Students experience the same challenges. When we assign homework tonight consisting of "problems 1 to 12 on page 152" and the assignment is due tomorrow, there is little doubt about where to write that assignment. The line or square representing that subject for today is the obvious place. When the assignment consists of interviewing a person in the community to learn about his or her vocation and the oral report will be presented two weeks from Thursday, what to write and where to write it becomes a bit more complex. Our job is to help students make the complex simple.

In this type of example, teach students to record all of this information on *today's* spot in their planners. When they get home, *today* is where they will look to see they have soccer practice. *Today* is where they will look to see the homework assignments they will complete tonight. *Today* also needs to be the place where they will see the larger and potentially ambiguous assignments that will need thought and planning in order to be carried out. That point will be explored in a moment as we look at breaking goals down into little parts.

Other Uses for the Student Planner

For the teacher seeking a great communication tool with parents, the student planner provides an outstanding low-tech option. The parent who does nothing more than simply look at the student's planner each night gains a wealth of information in terms of upcoming assignments and school events.

Often, a teacher needs to write a two-sentence note to a parent, yet knows that notes often find their way to the bottom of the book bag or get stuffed into a pants pocket. If the teacher writes those same two sentences on today's spot in the planner, the parent who examines the planner nightly is sure to see the teacher's comments and can respond with his or her own.

If planners are used as a schoolwide initiative, they can act as a student's hall pass at the middle or high school levels. Because the planner will be with the student in every class, the teacher need only write the time, destination, and add a signature on today's spot in the planner. This practice also lets parents see just how many times their student has asked to leave class. The teacher issuing the pass can also quickly see if the student has already been excused during other classes earlier in the day.

Ray Cheshire, a science teacher in the United Kingdom, has found a way to use student planners to check student understanding. Their planners have various sections that are preceded by a colored divider. Students are asked to hold up their planners with the green divider showing to indicate they understand the point Mr. Cheshire is making and hold up the orange divider to indicate they do not understand. If the front and back covers of the planner look decidedly different, holding up the planner with the front showing could indicate understanding while holding up the planner with the back showing could indicate not understanding. Ray says that by getting the students to hold their planners in the air, he has visual feedback of their understanding. He also uses this tool in debates or when voting.

Break Goals Down into Little Parts

As adults, we remember fondly the English teacher who not only helped us plan, but *made* us plan. She assigned the term paper and told us it would be due in two months. However, she went on to say, "I want you to turn in your topic this Friday, your outline the next Friday, and a dozen note cards the next Friday." That teacher knew that left to our own devices, we would put off the seemingly overwhelming job until the last minute and then throw something together quickly. She made us break the big job into manageable parts.

What are the big projects or goals for our students? Perhaps making the Accelerated Reader "100 Point Club," earning that badge in scouting, or making a sports team rank among the goals our students are trying to achieve. For each one, there is a set of steps. When the little steps are defined and handled, the big projects fall into place. Goals become reality.

The student planner is the perfect tool for project planning. We must teach students to trap the "big idea" on today's spot in the planner. Then we can start at the end and work backward. Begin by having students turn to the date the big project is due. Put that due date in the planner. Have students think through the steps along the way, assign a target date for each, and enter them in the planner. Before you know it, the entire project will be mapped in the planner. As the old saying goes, "The journey of a thousand miles begins with a single step."

The process just described is one that all too many adults fail to grasp. Goals remain large, undefined, and unaccomplished. This process is not natural; it must be taught. In time, students catch on to the ability to think through the steps and write them down. The journey starts, however, with a teacher who models this process time and time again.

Empty the Book Bag Totally Every Night

For some students, the book bag is a big black hole into which papers go and are never seen again. When the student finally cleans out the book bag in May, one can only imagine what lurks at the bottom. That permission slip he never could find, the homework paper he was sure he completed, and that half-eaten banana are among the treasures waiting at the bottom of the bag.

Insist that when students get home, they empty their book bags *totally*. After all, everything in there was packed for a reason, or at least hopefully so. Everything was something the student thought would be needed at home. The idea needs to be that we empty the book bag into one big pile and start to work through it. If the math book was brought home to complete an assignment, go ahead and get the assignment knocked out. The math book can then go back in the bag. If the stack includes papers for the parents, those papers need to be moved to a spot the students and parents agree is a good place for papers which need their attention. I cover this point in more detail shortly.

The problem so many students face is that they put items in the book bag that do not necessarily need to be taken home. They load the bag with every book in the desk simply out of habit. The result is a book bag that is heavier than it needs to be. Emptying the book bag and then handling every item in the pile quickly identifies anything that has gotten a "free ride" home. This practice also insures that students are not losing items in the bag. Finally, they will not be carrying items back and forth each day that should have gone in a trash can long ago.

Learn to Deal with Papers

So much of the information exchanged between home and school happens through written communication. Report cards, weekly folders, notes from teachers, field trip permission forms, and newsletters are examples of information that comes via paper. Some students seem to have no problem getting papers home and back on time. Other students never seem to be able to get anything home. Papers get wadded in pockets, stuck inside textbooks or notebooks, or placed inside desks. By the time the student gets home, where to find that paper is anybody's guess. Having a simple plan puts an end to a great deal of unnecessary stress.

Students need a place at school to put the papers to be delivered to Mom or Dad and put them there every time. Some classes may have a special folder that goes home each night. If not, sliding the papers in the planner right at this week's page will work. When the student opens the planner at home, he is automatically looking at the papers, an instant reminder that they need to be handed off to Mom or Dad.

Students also need a spot at home where papers for Mom or Dad will be placed. The last thing a parent needs when getting home from a busy day at work is to have a fistful of papers shoved at him. Nor does Mom need to go on a safari through the home looking for papers that may have been scattered in the most unlikely of places. Conducting an excavation inside a book bag is no fun either.

Children don't have it any easier. They don't always know when parents are ready to focus on papers from school. Having one spot to put everything for Mom or Dad's review makes life easier for all concerned. That spot may be a letter tray just inside the front door, a designated spot in the kitchen, or any other place, so long as both parent and student are consistent in its use.

Get Everything Ready the Night Before

Forgotten items, missed school busses, and frazzled nerves can so often be traced back to one simple problem—assuming "Rome can be built" between the time the alarm clock sounds and the school bus pulls up to the curb. Morning is a *terrible* time to finish that last bit of homework, complete that poster, or get those papers signed. Without fail, that book we just knew was on the coffee table is nowhere to be found and it's already time to pull out of the driveway.

Students can make the decision on what they will wear the next day and have the attire already laid out. They can pack the book bag before going to bed. They can gather anything else going to school and place it beside the book bag. In the morning, leaving the house is a simple matter of grabbing the book bag and whatever is around it, and heading out the door. Get *everything* ready the night before and mornings become more peaceful.

Organize the Locker

The locker becomes an important part of the school environment beginning usually with middle school. An organized locker means fewer lost or forgotten items. An organized locker also means less time spent with the locker and more time to spend in conversation with friends, an important part of student life.

Kerry Palmer is the middle school principal at Trinity Presbyterian School (Montgomery, Alabama). With lockers for sixth and seventh graders located directly outside his office, Mr. Palmer offers these practical suggestions based on his work with students in his school:

- ◆ Line up textbooks from left to right in the order they will be used during the school day.

- ◆ Have a "locker plan," a schedule of when to visit the locker each day. Students need not visit the locker every period. Gathering materials for two or three classes means less time at the locker and more time for socializing, visiting the restroom, and making it to class before the tardy bell.

- ◆ Determine what will be needed at home each evening by making notes in the planner. Students may then refer to the planner and retrieve the needed books before leaving for the day.

- ◆ Post the daily schedule on the inside of the locker door. This suggestion is particularly important if the school uses a rotating schedule where the order of classes changes from day to day.

- ◆ Keep the locker combination in a safe place. Forgetting the combination over a long break is common.

- ◆ Periodically clean out the locker so that it remains free of clutter.

In addition, locker dividers provide an inexpensive way to use more vertical space. The locker divider provides a *shelf* so that some items rest on the floor of the locker while other items rest on the shelf.

Use the "One-Binder Method"

The more folders, notebooks, and envelopes a student has, the more opportunity exists to misplace and forget those items. As an elementary principal, my upper elementary teachers loved the "one-binder method." Each student had one three-ring binder. A set of dividers separated the various subjects. Students used loose-leaf paper in the binder.

What are the advantages of this method?

- ◆ Students keep up with only one notebook. If they have their three-ring binder, they have *everything*.

- ◆ Pages are easy to insert and remove.

- ◆ With the use of a hole punch, students can include handouts in their binders.

- ◆ One binder takes up less room in lockers.

Maintenance of the binder will require some guidance from the teacher. Purging the binder at various points in the year will keep it from becoming overstuffed and ensure that this tool contains only papers which are relatively current. At the end of the grading period, or some other convenient points in the year, set aside time in class to instruct the student on what papers to remove from each divider section and which ones to leave in the binder. Papers removed from the binder go into a file folder labeled with the student's name and subject. As the teacher, you will keep those file folders. On the next purging day, distribute the same folders again.

This process of purging and filing accomplishes several objectives:

- The binder remains thin enough to be practical.

- The older papers stay in better shape because they are not being transported to and from school each day and are not being transported from class to class every day of the school year.

- The folders provide immediate access to examples of student work for each subject and for various points in the year.

- Assembling a student portfolio as the end of the year approaches becomes easy.

- Teachers are helping students learn an important life skill. Periodic purging and the organizing of archived material pays dividends in the workplace and in the home.

At Raymond L. Young Elementary School (Talladega, Alabama), Principal Pattie Thomas instituted the *TIGER* book in kindergarten through sixth grade. The name has a dual purpose. First, the school mascot is the tiger. Second, *TIGER* is an acronym for *Today I've Got Everything Ready*. Contents of this binder are as follows:

- Students in grades 3 to 6 have a student planner that is already hole-punched and placed in the binder.

- In grades K to 2, each child has a pouch for money.

- All students have a teacher/parent communication log.

- A copy of the school calendar is included.

- A designated section provides students a place to put homework and graded which needs to be either completed or given to parents.

Mrs. Thomas calls the *TIGER* book "a catch-all for home/school connection." She went on to say, "There are no excuses for unsigned papers, notes not seen, homework incomplete. It's all there."

School's Out for Summer

The final purge takes place at the end of the year. What happens to all of those papers created throughout the year? Do we save it all? Does it all go in the trash? Or, is there another alternative between the two extremes? This end-of-year purge is an opportunity to teach students a skill they can use throughout life—recognizing what has only temporary value, what has lasting value, and how to get rid of the former so that one can find the latter.

Most of what is produced during the year will be of little or no lasting value. On the other hand, such items as major writing projects and graphic organizers explaining important concepts in simple terms are worth saving. For the high school student, class notes provide valuable study guides to prepare for college entrance tests.

At the end of the year, the file folders come out one final time. At this point, the decision is not what comes out of the three-ring binder and goes into the folder. The decision to be made is what comes out of both the binder and folder to be thrown away and what will remain in the folder as a lasting artifact of the year's work for that subject. If the school maintains a portfolio on each student, certain items will be selected for the portfolio. The remainder of the folder goes home with the student at the end of the year.

What happens to it all from there becomes a family decision. Some well-chosen items will wind up in a scrapbook. Some photographs, artwork, or certificates may be framed. Students and their families are making decisions about what to toss, what to keep, and how to organize and display what is kept. In a world where we have far more paper in our lives that we can manage, the ability to make decisions about schoolwork is a prelude to making similar decisions about the paper and bulk items which will come their way in the adult world.

United We Stand

In the lower elementary grades, students have *one* teacher. They have *one* set of expectations. They have *one* set of procedures. As students move into the upper elementary grades, some changing of classes takes place. In the secondary grades, having multiple teachers is universal. When a student has seven teachers, the potential exists for that student to have seven sets of expectations and seven sets of procedures. Life is harder for the student, and life is harder for each of the seven teachers. There is an easier way, and all it takes is a little communication.

Should students put their names in the upper right corner of the page or the upper left corner? Should they put the date on the next line followed by the subject on the third line, or should it be the other way around? Which way should they fold their papers? The answer is that *it does not matter*.

What *does* matter is that teachers come to a *common decision*. When procedures are the same in every class the student enters, each teacher is reinforcing those procedures and making life easier for all of the other teachers. More importantly, consistency from classroom to classroom makes life easier for the students.

How will the three-ring binders be organized? In what order will the subjects appear in the binder? On what dates will the binders be purged in all classes? What will be done with the archived papers? What information will students put in planners? How will the program be monitored? These questions are not hard, and there is no single correct answer to any of them. The point is that these questions must be asked and answered. Otherwise, students are pulled in as many as seven different directions. We owe them more than that.

Conclusion

Time management and organization are challenges in the adult world. The mantra often heard is, *Nobody teaches this in school*. We can, and we should. Our world is complex. The world in which our students will spend adulthood will surely be far more complex. If people are to have the tools to handle the multiple projects and demands on their time, someone must teach them. Since these concepts do not fit neatly into the area of language arts, math, science, or social studies, no teacher sees teaching time management and organization as his or her responsibility. In the world of tomorrow, these are skills too important not to be taught.

Next Steps

- If you are departmentalized, schedule a meeting with colleagues to discuss the use of planners, the one-binder method, and other procedures that could be handled consistently across classrooms.

- Decide how you will fund planners. Choose a company and design.

- Review the supply list being sent to parents. Be sure that it includes the three-ring binder, dividers, and any other needed items for the one binder.

- Establish dates of "purge days" and put them on the calendar.

- Reread this chapter with attention to when each concept will be taught and when it will be reviewed.

♦ Schedule time during meetings with colleagues to discuss use of planners, progress with the one binder, and organization of purge days.

8

Organizing Your Computer

I do not fear computers. I fear the lack of them.
— Isaac Asimov

Our culture has trouble filing and finding paper after centuries of experience dealing with it. We should not be surprised to find many teachers totally lost when attempting to organize files on the computer. The problem which results is an inability to trust any type of digital filing/retrieval system.

Setting Up a Digital Filing System

Take a moment to see if you could answer "true" for each statement as it relates to that metal filing cabinet in your classroom:

☐ *I know where the box of file folders is kept.* You would have quite a time organizing a filing cabinet with no folders!

☐ *I know how to label (or relabel) a blank file folder.* Could you imagine simply using whatever labels already happened to be on the folders from a previous use?

☐ *I have set up a logical filing system.* If not, you would be randomly tossing files into any drawer of the filing cabinet. It would be doubtful anything could be found later.

☐ *I pay attention to where I file things.* If not, consider everything in the filing cabinet lost.

☐ *I can find what I have filed.* If any of the above statements are false, by this point retrieval will pose problems.

☐ *I routinely file papers.* Those who let them stack up on top of the filing cabinet must sort through the entire pile.

☐ *I have copies of important papers.* Ideally, it would be nice to have copies of all of your important papers filed offsite. In practice, making copies of all important papers and storing them in another location is not practical.

The preceding statements range from trite to ridiculous. Each statement, however, has a counterpart in the digital world. By looking at the two side by side, we can begin to see the problem people have when it comes to organizing their computers.

♦ **Paper:** I know where the box of file folders is kept.

♦ **Digital Counterpart:** *I can make a new folder when I need to do so.* A workshop conducted for the clerical staff in a school system revealed not one single person the group knew how to perform this skill. Their ability to organize files on their computers was as great as what they would experience trying to organize a metal filing cabinet with no file folders.

♦ **Paper:** I know how to label (or relabel) a blank file folder.

♦ **Digital Counterpart:** *I know how to label or relabel a folder.* Without this small skill, one will never have folders that are descriptive of what is in them.

♦ **Paper:** I have set up a logical filing system.

♦ **Digital Counterpart:** *I have set up a logical filing system.* Just as the absence of a logical filing system with a metal filing cabinet makes finding anything a challenge, the same is true on the computer.

♦ **Paper:** I pay attention to where I file things.

♦ **Digital Counterpart:** *I pay attention to where I file things.* Many people allow the computer to save files wherever it wants. *You* need to be the one making the decisions.

♦ **Paper:** I can find what I have filed.

♦ **Digital Counterpart:** *I can find what I have saved.* Just as with paper, if problems exist with any of the preceding statements, problems will exist here as well.

- **Paper:** I routinely file papers.

- **Digital Counterpart:** *I routinely clear my desktop.* You probably know people whose entire computer desktop is covered with icons, and even have icons sitting on top of other icons. You may even *be* one of these people. When one is looking at *everything*, it becomes hard to find *anything*.

- **Paper:** I have copies of important papers.

- **Digital Counterpart:** *I have a good backup routine and backup regularly.* The number of people who have no backup system is amazing. One hard drive failure is all that is required for years of data to be lost.

After reading this chapter, you will be able to answer "true" to every one of those statements as it pertains to your digital filing system.

The Desktop

The starting point is the desktop and making decisions about what can stay there. For some people, the answer is *everything*. The whole desktop is full of icons, with icons sitting on top of other icons. Limit the icons on the desktop to:

- "My Documents."

- Any program you use all day every day, such as Word, Outlook, or the school administrative software package.

- "Fingertip Files." These are those *few* files that you use very regularly. This concept will become clear later in the chapter.

- "Current Projects." This concept will also be explained later in the chapter.

- The Internet browser.

My Documents

The My Documents folder is the heart of the system. Depending on the operating system or platform, this folder is also called Documents. Think of it as the filing cabinet where you will to store all of the work you create. To begin organizing My Documents, look first at your paper filing system. Earlier, we discussed tidying up that system. Once you are pleased with the paper filing system, create a *comparable* system on the computer. For example, if a science teacher was handed a good lesson plan on photosynthesis, the teacher would need to have a place in the filing cabinet for it. If the same teacher was given a PowerPoint presentation on photosynthesis, the teacher should have a place in the digital filing system to put that PowerPoint presentation.

Having a model often serves as a good starting point. Figure 8.1 provides an example of the folders in a typical My Documents. Feel free to pattern your own system after this one. Alter it to fit your particular situation.

Figure 8.1. Sample My Documents Folder

Creating, Naming, and Renaming a Folder

When creating a filing system, you need to know how to create new folders. The steps for doing so are as follows:

1. Right-click in the My Documents folder (if that's where you want it to go). On a Macintosh, pressing the Control key and clicking gives the same result.

2. A menu appears.

3. Choose New.

4. When you highlight New, one of the options is Folder (Figure 8.2).

Figure 8.2. Creating a New Folder

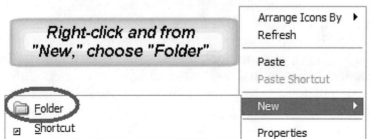

5. You will see your new folder. The title will be highlighted. Type the name for the folder (Figure 8.3).

Figure 8.3. Newly Created Folder

6. If a folder needs to be renamed, right-click on the folder and choose Rename. The name will be highlighted (as shown in Figure 8.3), and a new name for the file may be typed.

Saving Documents Logically

How often do you dread saving documents for fear of never being able to find them again? Many people opt to print a hard copy in case they cannot find their work on the computer. When changes need to be made, they wind up rekeying the entire document.

When saving a document, a dialogue box appears and tells exactly where the file is going to be saved. Figure 8.4 provides an example. By clicking Save, the file would be assigned the title shown in the File name line and be saved in the spot shown in the Save in line. In this example, the file would be saved under the name "Very Important Document" and would be found in the My Documents folder.

Figure 8.4. Saving a Document

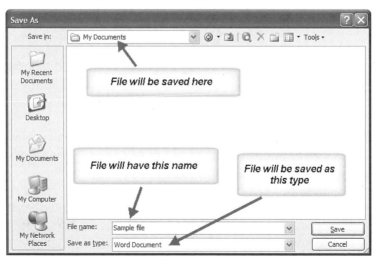

My Documents may be the desired location for the file. Then again, this location may not be the appropriate one. If the document is to be saved in one of these folders shown in the window, double-clicking on that folder will put that file name in the Save in line.

If you become puzzled, the easiest thing to do is just back up to the top level. Simply click on this folder with the *up* arrow until it won't go any further. Desktop will appear in the window. Then, choose whether you want to save it on the desktop. From there, drag the file into the appropriate file.

Memos and Letters

One of the folders I have in My Documents is called Memos & Letters. After composing a memo or letter, resist the temptation to save a paper copy of everything. Instead, electronically file any type of correspondence in the folder called Memos & Letters. The key to finding these documents later is to develop a system for naming files.

My preference is to name files with the last name of the recipient, followed by a hyphen, followed by several words that describe the subject matter of the document. Likewise, when receiving a document in digital fashion, I name the file with the sender's last name, a hyphen, and a few words descriptive of the subject matter.

For example, if writing to someone asking for their thoughts on playground equipment, there is no need to wonder weeks later when retrieving it whether the letter was named "Playground Letter," "Thoughts," or "New Playground." The document is going to start with the last name of the person, a hyphen, and several words related to the playground. Furthermore, it is going to be in the Memos & Letters folder, which is located in the My Documents folder.

Monthly Ticklers

Another notable folder I have in My Documents is called Monthly Ticklers. Education is a cyclic business. We find ourselves engaged in the same projects at the same time each year. In many cases, a project involves updating the forms and other paperwork that goes with it.

How nice would it be if all of the routine paperwork which we need to update during a given month was located in one place? The Monthly Ticklers folder is designed for just this function.

Inside the Monthly Ticklers folder are twelve folders labeled with the twelve months of the year. Each file contains the documents that need to be updated during that month. For example, a teacher's August folder might contain the "welcome to my class" letter and outline of the presentation for parents during Open House. At the first of August, the teacher opens the

August folder. Seeing the welcome back letter and outline serve as reminders to update and print these two documents.

An annual holiday production may be part of a teacher's activities each December. An introductory letter regarding that production may be found in the October folder. A draft of last year's program could be found in the November folder. A letter inviting the superintendent to attend the production and a request for the media to cover the event might be found in the November or December folder. Opening one of the monthly ticklers serves as the trigger to examine, update, and print each item there.

As one example, in the heat of the busy holiday season, how easy would it be to simply forget to drop the superintendent a letter of invitation? How embarrassing would it be for the teacher when the superintendent is asked about his absence from the program and replies that nobody told him anything about it? Having last year's invitation letter in the November file serves as the trigger to send this year's letter. A two-second date change and execution of the print command is all that is necessary to take care of the superintendent's invitation. Hurt feelings and social slights are not necessarily the result of not caring. Instead, they can and do result from people who are caring, yet overwhelmed, because they lack systems for handling the details.

Fingertip Files

Most people will find that 5% of their files account for 95% of the usage. Having those files where they are easy to access is a time saver paying dividends on a daily basis. Here are some examples of such files:

- ◆ Letterhead
- ◆ Memo Template
- ◆ Fax Cover
- ◆ Purchase Order Form
- ◆ Financial Spreadsheet
- ◆ Expense Form
- ◆ Meeting Planner

I handle these frequently used files by creating a folder on the desktop called Fingertip. It contains those few files that receive constant use. Double-clicking on that one folder puts the collection "at my fingertips."

Current Projects

The Current Projects folder is a place for all of the digital information related to a project in progress. My Current Projects folder resides on the desktop. Every item in the Current Projects folder is linked to the task list. On the task list, I place a *(CP)* beside a task that has supporting material in the Current Projects folder.

When I complete a task or a project that has the *(CP)* beside it, whatever was in the Current Projects folder must go somewhere else. Digital project information is treated just like the paper project information material housed in the tickler files. When the project is complete, a decision must be made as to what project information needs to be retained and what can be deleted. If the material is of lasting value, I "clean up" the digital material, getting rid of any individual documents not needed. I then drag the material into the digital reference system in My Documents.

Backing Up Your Files

"How many of you have a good system for backing up your files?" When this question is asked of a typical group of professionals, few if any hands are raised. When defining what is meant by a "good system" of backing up, it must be one that is *easy enough that you will actually do it*.

Before discussing a backup system, one must realize that basically two types of hard drives exist:

1. Those that have crashed.

2. Those that will crash.

These sobering thoughts should set the tone for wanting to learn and apply a good backup system.

To put the importance of this skill in perspective, examine what would happen if your hard drive were to crash today. With one phone call, you could probably summon the help of someone with the technical skills to get the computer up and going again. The job would entail purchasing and installing a new hard drive. This part is relatively inexpensive. The operating system resides on a set of CD-ROMs that came with the computer. Your tech-savvy friend can reinstall the operating system. The programs that were on the computer also can be reloaded from CD-ROMs. You can now resume using your computer just as you had before.

But can you? Where are all your documents? Without a good backup system, your documents are lost along with your hard drive. Without a good backup system, consider what will be *lost forever*:

1. *Beginning-of-year letter, grading information, and outline for the year*—Do you really want to be faced with having to rekey these entire documents?

2. *The entire whole packet related to that big field trip you sponsor every year*—Gone is the introductory letter, the release forms, the itin-

erary, the lesson plans preparing the students for the trip and providing followup activities after the trip. All of the well-crafted material that you had honed over the years is now history!

3. *Your term paper*—You have been working on that paper for your graduate class every night for the last three weeks, not to mention spending all of last weekend on it. The paper is due the day after tomorrow. Imagine the feeling of panic at having to re-create the paper from scratch.

With so much importance resting on our data, why do more people not have a system for protecting it from disaster? For the vast majority, the answer is easy. *Nobody ever showed them how.* Even if one tried to do a backup, what exactly would need to be copied? The computer has hundreds of thousands of files. Where would one even begin?

The answer is very simple. During the discussion throughout this chapter on setting up a digital filing system and saving files, where have we talked about saving them? The answer is exactly three places:

1. My Documents

2. Fingertip

3. Current Projects

Because you are only saving to those three places, you only have to back up those three files!

The following procedure provides a system that ensures your data is safe. In addition, it is easy enough *you will actually do it*:

1. Insert a flash drive or cable connected to an external hard drive into a vacant USB port.

2. Double click on My Computer. Your screen will look like Figure 8.5.

Figure 8.5. Backing Up Files

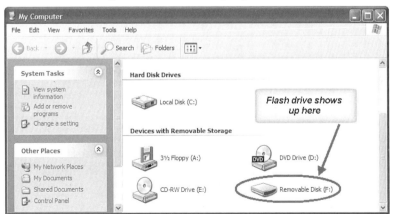

3. Double-click on the picture of the flash drive or external hard drive. The contents of the device will be displayed. There may not be anything on it or there may be some other files saved previously.

4. Create a new folder inside the backup device (Right-click > New > Folder). Name it with the current month and year. Double-click on that folder to open it.

5. Double-click on My Documents. You are now looking at two windows. One, My Documents, contains all of your files. The other, the folder on your flash drive or external hard drive, is the place where the files will be copied. Hold down the Control key and press the A for All.

6. All of the documents will be highlighted. Figure 8.6 provides an example of how these two folders may appear.

Figure 8.6. Folders Ready for Copying

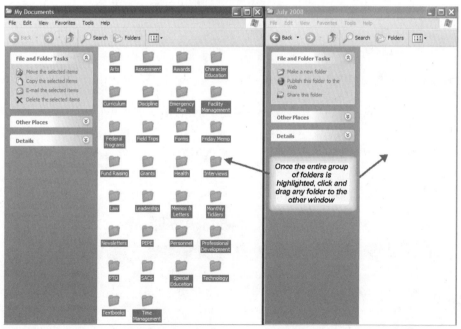

7. Click on any *one* of those files and drag it into the window where they will be copied. All of the rest of the documents will follow. As the files are copying, you will see a box with pieces of paper flying across from one folder to another (Figure 8.7).

Figure 8.7. Files Being Copied

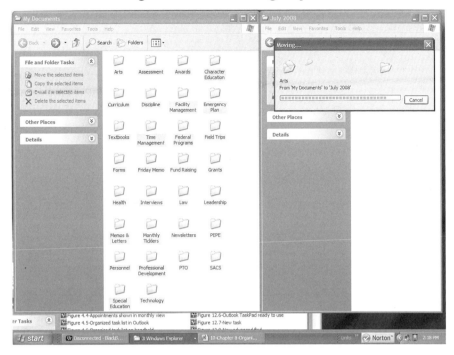

At this point, simply repeat the process with the "Fingertip" file and "Current Projects" file. The process is complete.

How often should this backup routine occur? There is no one answer. I backup My Documents once per month and backup both Fingertip and Current Projects weekly. If I were working on one document for an entire day or more, I backup that particular document at the end of the day.

Once you become comfortable with this process, it will become intuitive. Open a window for where your data is now. Open a window for where the data needs to go. "Select all" and drag. It does not get any easier than that!

Many school districts have systems in place where teachers store documents to a shared drive and a technology specialist is charged with backing up all data each evening. Such a system relieves the teachers of this duty. But, what about the teacher's home computer or laptop which may not be connected to this shared drive? The responsibility for protecting this data rests squarely with the teacher, and the technique described in this chapter will mean the difference between an inconvenience versus a major data loss should a hard drive fail.

As this chapter concludes, these points will be true about your computer if you follow the advice given:

1. You can file easily and logically.

2. You can find it later.

3. You are not going to lose it all if the hard drive crashes.

Now you have a system you can trust!

Next Steps

- Examine your paper reference filing system for any needed re-organization.

- List the digital files you will need for your digital reference files.

- Create all of the needed files in My Documents.

- Drag all of the documents currently on your computer to their proper folders within My Documents.

- Create your Fingertip and Current Projects files on the desktop. Drag to those files any documents which belong there.

- Decide what you will use to backup your files and secure whatever you will need.

- Include an entry in your "Repeating Task System" to remind you to backup your files.

- Include an entry on your "Repeating Task System" each month to remind you to check the Monthly Tickler.

9

E-Mail, the Digital Resources Chart, and Other Electronic Timesavers

Don't say you don't have enough time. You have exactly the same number of hours per day that were given to Helen Keller, Pasteur, Michelangelo, Mother Teresa, Leonardo da Vinci, Thomas Jefferson, and Albert Einstein.

— H. Jackson Brown

E-Mail: Time Management Tool or Time Sink?

For some, e-mail is a great timesaver; for others, it is a source of stress that consumes far too much time. Little more than a decade ago, the teacher who had e-mail at school was on the cutting edge. Now, the question is not *whether* a teacher has an e-mail address, but rather *how many*. We all love it, because it is easy to send a message to one person or to hundreds of people all with a single mouse click. We hate it, because our mail explodes with advertisements, jokes, and a host of other low-priority items. We stress about it because we also get good information and do not know exactly what to do with it.

E-mail is the most efficient means of communication available in the world of education. Even if phones existed in all classrooms, statistics from the business world show that something in the neighborhood of 20% of calls are completed the first time. With e-mail, messages are sent at a time convenient for the sender. They are read at a time convenient for the recipient. "Telephone tag" is gone forever.

In addition, e-mail allows the other party to do the necessary research *before* replying. We have all been caught off-guard by a telephone call where the caller asked for information we did not have available. E-mail eliminates the awkward game of "I'll get that information and get back to you."

Whether e-mail is a timesaver or time sink has little to do with the number of e-mails received. It has *everything* to with sound practice.

Decision, Decisions: Getting from "In" to "Empty"

Imagine for a moment a person has just arrived home from work. He walks to the curb and takes the mail from the mailbox. He opens the mail and reads it. He then walks back to the curb and *puts all of the mail back in the mailbox*. It sounds crazy, doesn't it?

The next day, when he walks to the mailbox, he finds today's mail sitting on *top* of yesterday's mail. After several more days, that mailbox will be so stuffed nothing else will fit. Even worse, he will hate that walk to the curb because he knows what mess awaits him.

This scenario sounds ridiculous, yet it is exactly how all too many people approach their *e-mail Inboxes*. They read a message, and because they don't know exactly what to do with it, they leave it. It is not uncommon to see an Inbox that contains every piece of e-mail the owner has received since the computer came out of the box! We would not stand for this situation with the mailbox by the curb. Why do we allow it for its digital counterpart?

When you walk away from that mailbox by the curb, it is *empty*. Better yet, it's not empty just *one* day. It is empty at the end of *every* day. How great it would be if only the e-mail Inbox operated that way?

The key to getting an empty Inbox is to *make simple decisions* about each and every item. Therefore, we must make it a practice to only look at e-mail when we have the time and energy to make those decisions. At that point, go from top to bottom and make those small decisions as each item is read.

Delete It

Much of the e-mail requires no action other than to briefly scan it and hit the delete key. Examples include advertisements of no interest, jokes, threads from e-mail discussion groups, and FYI courtesy copies. Many people find it helpful to sort the e-mail by *conversation*. All mail related to a single subject then appears together. If the subject is of no interest, delete the entire thread at one time.

Do It

Some e-mails require only a quick response. Give that response immediately and then delete the mail if it is of no further value. What if the response is going to take some time, and possibly some research? In that case, send a quick response to let the person know the message has been received and that you will be getting back with them. Using Outlook, drag the e-mail to the Task icon, assign a due date, and change the subject line as needed. Now, delete the e-mail.

Forward It

Perhaps someone else really needs to be handling this message. Simply forward the message to the appropriate person and delete the e-mail. If you should happen to need it later, go to "Sent Items" and view what had been forwarded.

Save It

What if the information might be of lasting value? This type of e-mail message poses more trouble than any other. We know the information might be needed again, but simply do not know what to do with it. Let's break the scenario down a little further and look at specific suggestions:

1. The text of the e-mail is of lasting value for documentation purposes—The reason for saving this information is so that it can be retrieved should someone ask for it. The value lies in lending proof of what was communicated and when. If you use Outlook to organize, drag the e-mail over the Notes icon. Edit the Note as need be and save. The Note is automatically date and time stamped upon creation. A second option is to save the e-mail in Memos & Letters in My Documents. To do this, go to the e-mail program's File menu and choose Save As. Navigate to the Memos & Letters folder and save.

2. The text of the e-mail is of lasting value because of the subject matter—For example, the text of the message contains sample

questions that you want to save for the next time you might interview for a position. Rather than save this message in the Memos & Letters folder, I would save it in My Documents in a folder labeled something like Career.

3. The e-mail has an *attachment* of lasting value for documentation—Drag the attachment to the Memos & Letters file. Rename the document with the name of the sender followed by a dash and a few words descriptive of the subject.

4. The e-mail has an *attachment* of lasting value because of the subject matter—Drag the attachment to the proper folder inside My Documents. If the attachment consisted of a set of interview questions, for example, drag it to the Career folder inside My Documents.

"In" Becomes "Empty"

The important point is that a decision is made about each piece of e-mail, and that decision is made the *first* time the message is read. Junk is *deleted*. Items requiring action either receive that action immediately or are added to the task list. In either case, the e-mail is then *deleted*. Items for someone else's attention are forwarded to them, and then *deleted*. Material to save is saved as a Note in Outlook, saved in Memos & Letters, or saved at some other appropriate place in My Documents. The message is then *deleted*. Soon, *In* becomes *Empty*.

E-Mail and the School Culture

If a fire broke out in the school in the middle of second period, the principal would not dream of communicating that information to teachers through an e-mail message. On the other hand, if the principal wanted to change next month's faculty meeting from Tuesday to Thursday, she would hopefully not make that announcement over the intercom during the middle of second period and interrupt instruction in every classroom. Different situations call for different methods of communication.

E-mail works best in schools that make a conscious decision as to *what type of information* will be communicated using that medium. In particular, the expected response time is critical. A principal who routinely sends e-mails that ask for a response within the hour, forces teachers to check e-mail constantly. By the same token, if teachers are sending each other messages that require a semi-immediate response, they are unconsciously creating a school culture in which e-mail becomes a constant, all-day interruption. This situation described here is all too common in many schools, not by design, but through failure to develop a "best practice" in this area.

What would happen if school personnel used e-mail only in cases where no action had to be taken the same day and no response was expected until the end of the day at the earliest? E-mail would become one less urgency in the lives of teachers. We could let it stack up during the day, give our full attention to the plans we had made for the day, and then handle all of the e-mail in one sitting at the end of the day.

Aside from reducing urgency, good e-mail practices eliminate fragmentation of communication. This point is particularly applicable when one person routinely communicates information to a group. When a thought occurs, we quickly compose an e-mail and send it to the rest of the faculty. An hour later, we have another thought, and hence anther e-mail. The upside is that we get those thoughts off our minds and move the responsibility to the reader. The downside is the readers are stuck with a hodgepodge of random e-mails. The sender would be much better off collecting those thoughts, organizing them into a well-crafted one-page piece of communication, and sending the finished product. Use of a blog, as described later in this chapter, offers an organized alternative to those random e-mails.

Delegating by E-Mail

Often, the purpose of an e-mail message is to ask someone else to do something. The ball is in the other person's court, but we still have the obligation to followup and ensure the other person delivers.

A simple technique for followup is to send yourself a copy of the message. Every e-mail program has in addition to the *to* and *cc* lines a line called *bcc*, which stands for "blind courtesy copy." The difference between the *cc* and *bcc* is significant. When an address is placed in the *cc* line, all other recipients can see that this person received a copy. When an address in placed in the *bcc* line, the person receives copy of the message, but no other recipient knows it.

When delegating a task to someone else via e-mail, simply put yourself in the *bcc* line. The next time you check your e-mail, a copy of that message arrives in the Inbox and serves as a reminder to follow up.

For those familiar with composing "rules" in Outlook, I have a shortcut that accomplishes this same purpose. One of the rules I have written looks for the tilde sign (~), which is located on the keyboard just the left of the numeral 1. If the tilde appears anywhere in the message, a copy of that message is placed in my Inbox.

What do you do with that reminder? Drag the e-mail over the task icon, which automatically creates a new task in Outlook with all of the appropriate information completed. Assign a due date, assign a status of "Waiting for someone else," and save. The e-mail message can be deleted. A reminder to follow up now resides on the Task list.

Sent Items: Your Permanent Record

One reason why I prefer e-mail over other forms of communication is that e-mail provides an instant record of what we have told other people and when we told them. By clicking Sent Items and typing a key word into the search box, you can put your hands on practically any message you have sent. The list can also be sorted by date or recipient, also allowing needed information to be found quickly.

Should there be any disagreement over what had been discussed via e-mail, referring to the Sent Items and forwarding to the other person a copy of the pertinent e-mail message clears up all doubt.

Minimizing Spam

Spam probably tops the list of things we hate about e-mail. Outlook is equipped with an excellent "spam filter." The filter identifies what it considers spam and presents it in a list of "junk e-mail." One can actually teach the filter to become more accurate. If the filter allows a message through from a sender whose mail you do not wish to receive, simply right-click on the message and choose "Add to Blocked Senders List." By the same token, if legitimate e-mail shows up in the junk mail, right-click on the message and select "Add to Safe Senders List."

Under no circumstances should anyone reply to spam asking to be removed from the sender's list. By replying to spam, one tells the spammer that he has hit upon a real e-mail address. Not only that, but the spammer knows he has found someone who is not only diligent about reading e-mail, but someone who responds to the e-mail received. Replying to spam makes the person a spammer's dream! Stand back and watch the Inbox overflow with spam! A better solution is to use the delete key and not give the spammers another thought. You have better ways to spend your time than to fume about spammers.

Be Part of the Solution by Not Being Part of the Problem

E-mail is the medium of choice for such time-wasting activities as forwarding jokes and hoaxes. Because sending to the entire address book is as easy as sending to a single individual, cyberspace is flooded with junk. I have made a personal decision to use the delete key. Although some of the jokes are funny and provide a good chuckle, forwarding them to a large group is something I choose not to do.

Gaining Newspaper Coverage

Do you feel your local paper is consistently there to cover the good things that happen in your classroom and school? Teachers are usually quick to lament the lack of coverage of the positive and the emphasis on the negative. My experience has been that newspapers are usually glad to print what is given them, *provided* it is delivered to the right person and the job is made easy for them. E-mail is the answer.

Telephone the paper and ask for the name and e-mail address of the person to whom school-related material should be sent. When newsworthy events happen, e-mail the story with an attached digital photograph to the appropriate person. This process eliminates the need to drive to the paper and search for the person who should receive this type of the material.

The newspaper reporter is relieved of the job of rekeying the copy into his computer. From his perspective, the job is a simple copy and paste from your e-mail and photograph to his computer. You have just made covering the good news happening in your school *easy enough the newspaper will include it*! Your story, along with the digital photo you include as an attachment, will most likely find its way into the paper.

Other E-Mail Tricks

1. *Check e-mail only at designated points in the day.* E-mail becomes an interruption and a time-waster when we check it constantly throughout the day.

2. *Handle all e-mail in one group.* Go from the top of the list and do not stop until you reach the bottom. Make a decision about each e-mail. Act on the e-mails that require action, or at least add items to your task list describing what needs to be done. Respond to those that simply need a response. Forward that which needs to be forwarded. File what needs to be filed. Delete what needs to be deleted. When you get to the bottom of the list, the Inbox should be empty.

3. *Delay checking e-mail until midmorning.* Begin the day with the tasks you had *planned* to begin your day. If you begin the day with e-mail, you may well get nothing else accomplished.

4. *Create subject lines that are descriptive of the message.* The person who receives your e-mail will be able to tell a great deal about the contents without even opening it. Whereas a subject line say-

ing "Meeting" conveys little, a subject line saying "Department meeting October 23 at 9:00 in the library" gives the receiver a much clearer picture of the nature and importance of the message. At times, the entire message in the subject line can be put in the subject line. "I found the book you asked for," "The figures you needed are attached," and "Can you meet with me Friday at 2:00?" are examples of how one can convey the entire message in the subject line.

5. *Keep messages short.* If at all possible, limit the message to one screen of text. If the message runs longer than that, perhaps several different subjects are being covered in the same message. If so, consider breaking the e-mail into several short messages, each handling a different subject.

6. *Front-load the message.* Begin by giving the reader an idea of what he will need to *do* about your message. Include the most important information towards the beginning of the message. Let the lesser important details bring up the tail end.

7. *Save time by creating a signature line.* The signature line can include anything you like. Typically, your name, title, organization, address, telephone, fax, and e-mail address are good information to include. The signature line is to the e-mail what letterhead is to written correspondence. Consulting the "Help" section of any e-mail program provides instruction on how to create a signature in that program.

8. *Avoid printing e-mail messages.* The advantage of digital data is the ease with which it can be stored, searched, retrieved, shared, or edited. When you print digital data, all of these advantages are negated. People often print e-mail because they are simply used to handling paper. Old habits can be hard to break.

The Digital Resources Chart

Good teachers have always sought additional resources to supplement what is supplied by the textbook. As a young teacher, I was hungry for the best ideas of how to teach particular concepts. When a good idea came my way, making a decision as to where in the students' development that idea should be introduced was the next step. Turning in the teacher's edition to that spot in the book and making note of that idea in the margins trapped the idea. If I had developed a handout to be introduced at a particular point in the year, turning to the appropriate page in my book and writing a note to pull the handout from the filing cabinet made that handout a part of my curriculum.

That strategy worked. Each year, I was assured that the ideas gained from workshops and the additional materials created would not be forgotten. Life was simple then.

Thanks to the Internet, access to resources has never been more plentiful. The situation, however, provides both a blessing and a curse. One Internet search returns page after page of hits. Handouts from any workshop will likely include a list of links to sites providing lesson plans, interactive activities, videos, and PowerPoint presentations.

Somewhere in that sense of euphoria surrounding the wonderful possibilities lies the gnawing reality that we are being introduced to more than we can possibly use. Euphoria can quickly turn into a sense of being overwhelmed. Realizing that we cannot assimilate it all, the tendency is to close the door to the possibilities, open the textbook, and let that textbook be the one and only resource. We can do better, and it's not that hard.

What if a teacher could have one chart listing all of the digital resources planned for use during the year. Suppose the chart is easy to edit so that new digital resources can be added in seconds. Suppose each item on the chart is hyperlinked to the digital resource, so that the teacher is only one mouse click away from that resource. For the teacher who has a "Digital Resources Chart," *overwhelmed* is a word that never enters into the picture.

Figure 9.1 shows the very top of what a Digital Resources Chart would look like for an elementary teacher. The chart consists of one spreadsheet. Across the top, the teacher lists the subjects being taught. Down the side is a timeline dividing the school year into small increments of time.

Figure 9.1. Digital Resources Chart

	A	B	C	D	E	F
1		Reading	Language Arts	Math	Science	Social Studies
2	Week 1	Anthem Sing Along	Contraction Interactive	Interactive Addition Game	Water Cycle Video	Indian Tribe Graphic Org.
3			Pronoun Dropdown	Mutiplication Facts Handout	Water Cycle PPT	Fact or Fiction?
4				2-digit multipli. PPT		

The teacher who is responsible for multiple subjects may wish to list the weeks of the school year down the side. Those who teach a single subject may wish to coordinate the labels down the side of the chart with the textbook. Instead of "Week 1," "Week 2," and so forth, this teacher may use labels such as "Chapter 1 Section 1," "Chapter 1 Section 2," and the like. Because the chart is maintained on an Excel spreadsheet, additional rows can be added or excess rows deleted with ease.

Maintaining the chart is similar to the process I used many years ago. Instead of a new resource being penciled in the margin of the teacher's edition, the teacher simply clicks on the appropriate cell, keys in the name of the new resource, and then turns that name into a hyperlink.

To illustrate how the process works, let's return to the Digital Resources Chart as it is shown in Figure 9.1. The teacher has found a good PowerPoint presentation consisting of "Fry Phrases," common phrases encountered by young children in their reading. In this PowerPoint, each phrase remains on the screen for several seconds before automatically advancing to the next one. The teacher believes this PowerPoint would be excellent to use during the first week of school during the reading block.

To add this PowerPoint to the Digital Resources Chart:

1. Click on the appropriate square, in this case, cell B3.

2. Key the term "Fry Phrases" and press the Enter key.

3. To create a hyperlink, right-click on the words "Fry Phrases."

4. A menu appears, and Hyperlink is one of the choices. Click on that choice (Figure 9.2).

Figure 9.2. Select Hyperlink

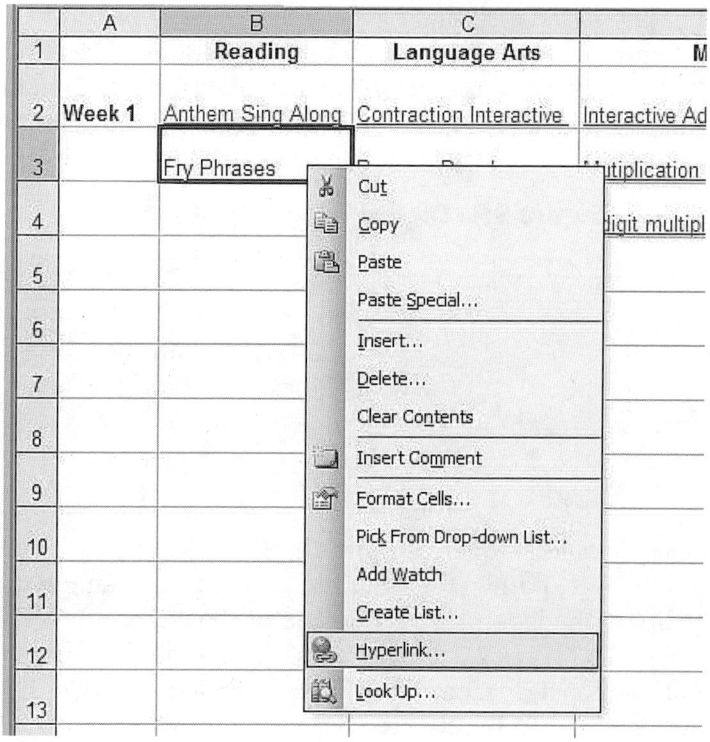

5. A box appears and asks for the address for where this resource is located.

6. If the resource is housed on the computer, navigate to that resource just as you would navigate to a document in order to attach it to an e-mail. Click OK (Figure 9.3).

Figure 9.3. Selecting the Path

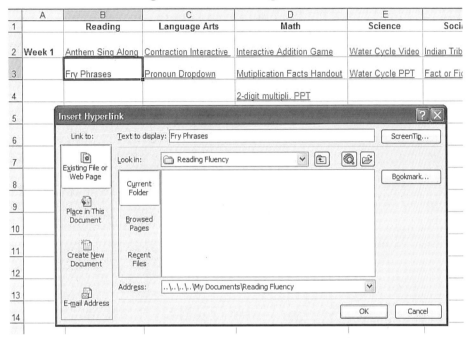

7. If your resource is housed on the Internet, key or paste the URL into the address window. Click OK.

8. A hyperlink has been created (Figure 9.4).

Figure 9.4. Hyperlink to the PowerPoint Presentation Created

	A	B	C	D	E	F
1		Reading	Language Arts	Math	Science	Social Studies
2	Week 1	Anthem Sing Along	Contraction Interactive	Interactive Addition Game	Water Cycle Video	Indian Tribe Graphic Org.
3		Fry Phrases	Pronoun Dropdown	Mutiplication Facts Handout	Water Cycle PPT	Fact or Fiction?
4				2-digit multipli. PPT		

9. Clicking on link opens the PowerPoint presentation.

What type of resources of resources can be listed on the Digital Resources Chart?

- ♦ Lessons plans housed either on the computer or Internet.

- ♦ Handouts, tests, or other written material housed either on the computer or Internet.

- ♦ PowerPoint presentations housed on the computer or Internet.

- ♦ Pictures housed on the computer or Internet.

- ♦ Videos housed on the computer or Internet.

Once the first teacher has composed a good Digital Resources Chart, the question will soon arise as to whether or not the teacher can share that chart with others. The answer is both "yes" and "no." The Excel spreadsheet can easily be copied onto any other computer. Any hyperlink that takes the user to a resource on the *Internet* will work from any computer. A hyperlink designed to go to a resource housed on the creator's *computer* will not work from other computers. If the hyperlink points to a resource on a shared drive, that link will work from any other computer sharing that same drive.

The Digital Resources Chart is a living chart where resources will constantly be added as they are discovered and others deleted as they outgrow their usefulness. It requires only that we make decisions on the front end as to exactly what point in our curriculum we will use each item. All of our digital resources are in one place, and each is a click away. Life just got easier!

Using Student Information System Software to the Fullest

As recent as a generation ago, schools managed administrative tasks by dividing them amongst the faculty and letting everyone share the load. Today, the student information system software has the capability to produce honor roll lists, average end-of-year grades, address envelopes, and conduct countless clerical tasks that were so time-consuming not so many years ago.

Many of today's administrators and teachers remember performing these clerical tasks during their early years in the teaching field. Unfortunately, many of these clerical tasks are still being farmed out to already overwhelmed teachers without stopping to consider how the software could accomplish the same tasks more accurately in a fraction of the time.

Many other schools, however, make their student information systems sing like a well-tuned violin. The difference between those who harness the power of this technology and those who do not seems to lie with the habit of asking one simple question. Before asking teachers to assimilate data or perform any of these other clerical functions, the savvy principal asks the question, "Can I get the computer to do this for me?" Teachers also must be willing to ask this question. The answer was usually "Yes." Asking the questions puts one half-way towards finding the answer.

Teachers who want to save time by letting the software do the work will benefit from these suggestions:

1. If you find yourself handwriting student data, *STOP!* Ask if the information can be produced by the software, and do not necessarily take "no" for an answer. When people say, "It can't be done," what they so often mean is, "I don't know how to do it."

2. Read the help guides. Makers of student information system software generally compose help documents covering each module of the program and make these available on their websites. You can read about grading, attendance, or student demographics, just to name a few. You will be surprised at the capabilities you would have never thought were present. Not only will these documents answer the questions you have, they will reveal answers to questions you did not know to ask. Uncovering one capability and sharing it with the main office could result in a tremendous time-saver for the entire building.

3. Utilize telephone technical support. The school probably pays an annual fee for technical support, so get your money's worth. Keep the telephone number handy. When a question arises, telephone the people whose business it is to know that piece of software forward and backward.

One example of holding on to practices of the past when a much more efficient practice exists today is in the area of collecting student demographic data at the beginning of the school year. The universally accepted method prior to around 1990 was to send a home a form printed on a large index card for parents to complete. That card would then be filed in the main office. Perhaps the school would send home several such cards. One would be filed in the office, another in the counselor's office, and a third might be kept by the homeroom teacher. If an address, telephone numbers, or names of persons allowed to check the child out from school had changed from the previous year, filling out new cards at the beginning of the year insured accurate data.

Today, when we need an address or telephone number, we look up the data on our computers rather than consult cards. However, many schools continue the same practice of sending home the annual index card as a means of keeping their data current. Using this procedure, the only way to be sure the information in the computer is accurate would be for someone to examine each piece of data on the card versus each piece of data on the computer. The task would be unreasonably labor intensive.

The solution to the problem is so simple. Prior to the opening day of school, the administrative assistant prints from the computer a demographic sheet for each student. Most school software packages have such a report already formatted. The parent is then asked to examine the sheet and mark prominently anything that has changed. The administrative assistant then simply flips through the forms looking for items parents have marked and makes corrections on the computer during the process. Once all corrections have been made, the demographic forms are retained for those times when the electricity may go out.

Search the Internet

Those of my generation grew up in a period when finding information was a time-consuming task. All but the most elementary research included getting in the car and driving to a large library, combing the card catalog, consulting the *Reader's Guide to Periodical Literature*, and then going on a safari through row after row of books to physically lay hands upon one book after another.

Research has become much easier, to say the least. One thirty-second online search garners more information than a week in the library. The improvement opportunity for many teachers is to make an Internet search our first thought. Yes, we may be able to uncover the same information by scouring books and periodicals in our offices. An Internet search often puts the same or similar information at our fingertips in seconds.

Searching the Internet for information is an exceptional timesaver when we need to have that information in digital format. Suppose one is preparing a newsletter and wishes to include a certain lengthy poem. Having the poem at hand, many teachers would key the lengthy poem into the computer. The tech-savvy teacher would let an Internet search find the poem. A single copy-and-paste puts the poem into the newsletter in seconds. Of course, one should be careful to obtain permission before using copyrighted material.

Teachers save time when they ask if the student information system software to give them needed data rather than having an entire team of teachers to collect it. By the same token, teachers save time for themselves and those around them when they first consider the search capabilities of the Internet before using less-efficient means of collecting data.

The Teacher's Blog

Short for "weblog," a "blog" is a quick-and-easy way for the teachers to have a presence on the Internet and communicate with his or her audience. A teacher's blog may communicate with students in the class as well as the parents of those students. The teacher may also use a blog as a means of sharing resources with colleagues across the world.

My own experience with blogging began as a followup to my workshops. The blog serves as a means to maintain contact with workshop participants long after the workshop had concluded.

During my final year as a principal, I created two blogs. One was designed to communicate with the staff, and replaced the paper memo I had used religiously since coming to that school. Each week, a new blog post would provide information the staff would need during the week. A second blog was used as a vehicle to communicate with parents. In this case, the blog replaced the paper newsletters I had been producing.

When I moved from the principalship to the central office, creating two blogs was one of the first orders of business. One was designed to provide news from our schools and central office to the community. The second was created to serve as a tool to communicate with all of our employees.

A blog offers these advantages:

- Blogs are easy to compose.

- The price is right. Many sites allow the user to establish a blog for free. No special software is required. An Internet connection is all that is needed.

- Blogs are easy to maintain. New posts appear at the top of the blog. Each post is automatically date and time stamped.

- You have an automatic history of everything you have posted. All previous posts are maintained in chronological order from the most recent to the most ancient.

- You can post pictures or videos. Any digital photograph or piece of digital clipart that can be downloaded to the computer desktop can be posted on your blog.

- You can insert links into any post. With one click, teachers or community members can be directed to any spot on the Internet you wish them to visit.

Next Steps

- Empty your e-mail Inbox using the method described in this chapter.

- Decide on your method for following up on items delegated by e-mail. Will you *bcc* yourself or write a "rule" that puts a copy of the e-mail in your Inbox?

- Sort your e-mail Inbox by "conversation." Right-click on the title bar and make your selection.

- Call your local newspaper to get the name and e-mail address of the proper person for school news. Put this contact information in your e-mail program.

- Find the telephone number for your student information system software technical support. Put this number in your signature tool.

- Locate the instruction manual for your student information system software. Add reading that manual to your task list.

- Examine the data you are being asked to gather. Determine how much of this information can be pulled from your administrative software. Make suggestions to your principal on ways paperwork can be lessened.

- Explore the blogs mentioned in this chapter to determine if you would like to start your own.

10

Focused or Fragmented?

If you know the point of balance,
You can settle the details.
If you can settle the details,
You can stop running around.
Your mind will become calm.
If your mind becomes calm,
You can think in front of a tiger.
If you can think in front of a tiger,
You will surely succeed.

— Mencius, Chinese Philosopher (372–289 BC)

For teachers, time is limited and the demands on that time seem unlimited. Finding time to work on the to-do list often means arriving at school early or staying late. The planning time is subject to interruption from drop-in visitors, phone calls, and new e-mail. Our days become fragmented. We leave in the evening feeling nothing has been accomplished and that we are further behind today than yesterday. That very feeling may be what prompted you to read this book.

To this point, this book has provided a system to organize papers, appointments, tasks, repeating tasks, documentation, and the computer. In short, the tools are in place to organize all of the obligations you have accepted. This chapter explores our ability to choose. We have the ability to say "no," "not now," and "not me" that is far greater than we realize.

Work from an Organized List

The old adage "plan your work and work your plan" is good advice for a busy teacher. Handling challenges as they appear does keep us busy; however, it is an inefficient and ineffective way to work. You have learned how to construct an organized task list that groups similar items together. Furthermore, you have learned how to make the list *crystal clear*. When looking at a task, you know exactly how to accomplish it. The list has a natural "flow."

The strategy we must develop in a world filled with interruptions is to work our list. Instead of allowing e-mail, cell phones, and drop-in visitors to derail our train of thought, we can use e-mail, voice mail, and human "gatekeepers" to trap incoming data. Later in the day, we look at all of the new inputs as a group and plan how to respond. Although the ringing and dinging of our digital interrupters gives the impression of urgency, the truth is that virtually all of them can wait.

Work from the list and you insure you are getting the most done in a given amount of time. You eliminate hopping back and forth between tasks. Few people realize how much time and energy is required to refocus on the work at hand once it is interrupted. The more you jump from project to project, the more time you waste.

Quiet Time

Statistics show that the average executive in the business world is interrupted anywhere from every three minutes to every eight minutes. Refocusing after an interruption may take fifteen minutes. Our profession is no different. With statistics such as these, is it any wonder we leave work feeling we have accomplished nothing?

But shouldn't we be always accessible for others? Imagine two people of similar ability. You know that you can call Person A at any time. E-mail him and receive a response within a few minutes every time. Drop in anytime and find an open door. To this point, the scenario sounds appealing. Realize, however, that when Person A is working on a project for *you*, this person stops to answer every phone call, respond to every e-mail, and see anyone who wishes to stop by for a chat. The project you thought would be completed quickly drags on for weeks.

Person B, on the other hand, is harder to access *immediately*. Person B returns your calls and e-mails within the day, but not within minutes. Yet, when working on a project for *you*, Person B is focused on that project and that project alone. It is completed accurately and in a timely fashion. Ask yourself two questions: Which person would you rather have working with you? Which person's time would you respect more?

To accomplish anything of substance, you must establish some uninter-rupted time. That time occurs before school, after school, during the allo-cated planning time, or a combination of all three. All of that is personal preference. Two points are crucial. One is that uninterrupted time is estab-lished. The second point is that a plan exists for how that time will be used. The organized task list keeps you focused on what has been planned for your time. Without it, distractions take hold, and a thirty-minute planning time is gone with nothing to show for it.

You can make carrying out your plans easier by having materials at hand. If grading a set of papers is the intent of your planning time, having them already assembled and placed in your pending tray increases the likelihood that they will be graded as planned.

Is duplicating papers on the to-do list? Unless a copier is available in the classroom, saving items to be copied and handling a number of them all in one group is a much better use of time.

Is a classroom-related errand on the list? Leaving campus during plan-ning time should be avoided at all costs. Invariably, the travel time there and back exceeds the time actually involved in the task. Group the errands and leave school a little earlier than normal one day to run them all at one time. Planning time is left intact for that which can be done in the classroom. Furthermore, the unexpected train, slow lines at the bank, or other variables always associated with errands will not impair being back in the classroom when students return.

You Teach Other People How to Treat You

When working on an important project and someone drops in, what do you do? If you drop the project and let this person have as much of your time as desired, get ready for a repeat performance. Do you respond to every e-mail as soon as it rolls in? If so, others will come to expect it and be upset in the event they do not receive a response instantly. Basically, you will teach those around you how to treat you by what you allow. Furthermore, you teach others how you value your own time by how well or poorly you man-age it.

When someone else waits until the eleventh hour and then drops a task in your lap, how do you handle the situation? Bail the other person out, and the lesson you teach is that others can wait until the last minute and you will still make sure everything turns out just fine. Prepare for more of the same.

Do you find yourself unable to tackle valuable tasks because you are an-swering insignificant questions posed in e-mail and handling other trite re-quests? If you continue to work through your organized task list and handle these interrupters last rather than first, interesting things begin to happen. People will try and find answers on their own before turning their research projects over to you. When they see that you have a plan for your time, they will find someone else to handle the trivial tasks.

Another side to this scenario exists. As you assume projects of significance and produce results, a clear message is sent that you are the person for this type of assignment. How do you wish to spend your time—on the trivial or on the significant? Ultimately, that choice is yours. You do teach people how to treat you.

As a faculty, you can come to some common agreement on how you will treat each other. How will the intercom be used? Will it be a vehicle for interrupting every lesson in the school throughout the day with trivial announcements and requests which could have been handled at another time? If so, lessons become fragmented with the time spent on the interruption plus the time spent recovering from that interruption. With a little planning, use of the intercom can easily be reduced to first thing in the morning and, if needed, last thing in the afternoon.

How will e-mail be used? Will it be used when an immediate answer is required? If so, teachers are forced to check it repeatedly throughout the day. Instead, if the common agreement is that e-mail will not be used if action is expected the same day, teachers can be comfortable in checking e-mail once each day and handling it all in one group.

How does the school handle drop-in visitors and phone calls? Are teachers routinely called to the phone simply because it happens to be their planning time? Is the drop-in visitors sent to a teacher's class because it happens to be the teacher's planning time? If so, planning time is fragmented, and nothing is accomplished.

If we agree that time is the vehicle through which we accomplish everything of substance, then we must develop a school culture where we respect the time of each other. Allowing out colleagues blocks of uninterrupted time is a gift we give them, and a gift that, hopefully, we receive in return. The result is that we accomplish more and can go home a little earlier.

How Much Can You Do Well?

We are capable of handling a great number of projects. We simply cannot work on all of them simultaneously. A large part of maintaining your sanity has to do with learning to say, "Not now." The signature tool is your friend when it comes to trapping those projects that you cannot accept now but want to accomplish in the future.

If you organize with paper, Chapter 4 discussed using a "Future Tasks" page in the back of the planner to record worthy tasks, projects, or goals that you cannot begin now. For those who organize digitally, add these items to the Task list and assign a date sometime in the future when you would like to consider them again. In either case, you can now concentrate on the task at hand. All of those other worthwhile projects will be waiting their turn.

Who Can Help? The Art of Delegation

Elementary school teachers are masters of delegation. One student is in charge of changing the calendar date. Someone else passes out papers. A third student is in charge of feeding the classroom hamster. The list goes on and on.

Elementary school teachers understand something so many of us miss. None of us can do everything. Others can do some of those things as well as we can. Sharing the load not only frees us to do those tasks that only we can do, it gives others a stake in the program.

Look for the repeating tasks. The routine things that must be done daily, each week, or each month serve as prime candidates for delegation. As others assume some of these tasks, your time becomes free for those things only you can do.

When we delegate responsibilities to students, we accomplish several goals:

- ◆ We reduce the time that we, as teachers, spend on nonteaching functions and give ourselves more time for that which is related to the craft of teaching.

- ◆ We give students a sense of ownership in the classroom.

- ◆ We teach responsibility. The classroom only functions efficiently when everyone does his or her job.

As a first step, think through the tasks that you are performing that a student could do as well, *or better*, than you. Jenny Cheifetz, who taught elementary school in New Hampshire, provides this list of possible jobs that students could perform:

- ◆ Pick up trash and sweep.

- ◆ Dust window sills.

- ◆ Water plants.

- ◆ Erase and clean board and organize tray.

- ◆ Straighten and clear tables.

- ◆ Organize and sweep rug area.

- ◆ Straighten homework bin area.

- ◆ Straighten bookshelves.

- Take attendance/lunch count.

- Serve as runner to bring messages to office and other teachers.

- Lead the recitation of the Pledge of Allegiance.

- Pull a CD for the music of the day.

- Serve as line leader.

- Pass out papers.

- Collect papers.

Pattie Thomas used a similar approach in her early childhood classroom at Raymond L. Young Elementary School (Talladega, Alabama). To give students ownership in running the classroom, every child had an "Adopted Area" of the room. At the end of the day, every child handled his or her "Adopted Area" at the same time. Mrs. Thomas noted the secret of the program's success was a three-minute timer. When she set the timer, all of the children went to work simultaneously. At the end of three minutes, the board was clean and ready for the next day, complete with tomorrow's date written in the corner. Plants were watered. Pencils were sharpened. Tables were wiped. The floor was swept. Books were straightened. Materials were arranged for the next day. All the while, Mrs. Thomas stood back and watched as the children took care of their "Adopted Areas." Teaching can be a stressful job. Master teachers find ways to reduce the stress.

Both Cheifetz and Thomas used a similar approach to organizing the system. A bulletin board in the room sported a set of library pockets, each pocket labeled with the name and possibly the picture of a specific job. Each child's name was written on a Popsicle stick. Both teachers talked about the importance of *every single student* having a job. Job assignments were made by simply putting the Popsicle sticks in the pockets. For bigger jobs, two or three students can be assigned to work together.

Rotating jobs was another important part of the program. Mrs. Thomas rotated her jobs every month, giving students a long enough period to learn the job and perform it well without becoming bored. Teaching the child how to perform his or her job at the "Adopted Area" was also important. Similarly, Ms. Cheifetz stated, "You can't expect a clean room if the students don't know your definition of clean."

Clearly, these examples are taken from elementary schools. If you are a secondary teacher, the same type of approach will work. Those who teach in this arena can ask themselves questions about the "housekeeping" duties present in the classroom. Examine them in terms of first period duties, last period duties, and duties that would be performed every period.

The first period, or homeroom, generally includes some type of procedure for taking attendance for the day and gaining an accurate lunch count.

Traditions such as reciting the Pledge of Allegiance or observing "a moment of silence" take place during this time. Memos or flyers intended for the entire student body are often distributed at this time. Likewise, material that the entire student body is expected to return is often collected at this point in the day.

Homeroom, or first period, is also a time when certain materials are set up to be used for the day. The projector must be turned on. The laptop to which that projector is connected must be booted. Activities that students will begin when they arrive in class at the beginning of each period must be written on the board. As a teacher, list the specific "housekeeping" duties you find yourself performing. This list is the foundation of your own "Adopted Area" system.

Likewise, the last period of the day is a unique time. It is the time when the day winds down, when things are put away, and when some preparation for the next day can happen. Again, think through the "housekeeping" tasks that are keeping you at school longer than necessary. Organize a system whereby you enlist the help of multiple students.

Finally, those tasks exist which occur every period. Papers must be collected. Papers must be distributed. The door must be closed when the tardy bell rings. Provisions must be made to save materials for students who are absent. The list goes on and will differ from teacher to teacher.

In his book *The Essential 55*, Ron Clark (2003) talks of delegating to various students tasks needed to set up the overhead projector. One student closed the blinds, another turned off the lights, another closed the door, another pulled down the screen, another wheeled the projector in place, and another plugged it into the wall. By simply saying, "Let me show you that on the overhead projector," the whole process was set into motion and completed by the time it took him to pick up his overhead pen.

Make your own list. Then, make your plan for how you will delegate these tasks to students, how you will rotate the jobs, and how you will quickly and effectively teach the students how to perform the duties well. Yes, teaching has the potential to be a very stressful job. The organized teacher realizes that thriving in this field includes being good to yourself. Allowing students to help share the load is not a sign of laziness. Far from it, the practice builds responsibility and a sense of ownership among the students. It promotes a sense of "family" within the classroom. Best of all, it provides more time for the teacher to teach.

Turn Off the Flood

A common concern among teachers is staying on top of the mountains of papers to grade. Although we often fail to realize it, the good news is that we are the ones who decide what to assign, when to assign it, and how it will be graded. The following suggestions are designed to help minimize the paper avalanche:

♦ You need not grade everything that is assigned. Let students know that although their assignments often will be graded for accuracy, at other times they will simply be awarded credit for submitting the assignment.

♦ You need not grade all parts of what is assigned. If twenty examples are assigned, you might grade only the second ten.

♦ When assigning a grade is unimportant, allow students to check their own papers or exchange papers with a neighbor during class.

♦ Use available technology, such as student response systems, to grade understanding instantly and without creating more paper.

♦ Enlist the help of an aide or parent to assist with the grading of papers.

♦ Examine the purpose for giving assignments. To assign work just because it has been traditional to give an assignment every night is a poor use of both student time and teacher time.

Every school has its own rules that may limit the flexibility that a teacher has. For example, check with the principal regarding allowing a parent volunteer to grade student work. What will be seen as no problem in one community may be a big problem in another community because of a past uncomfortable situation.

Often, the subject of privacy comes into play when a teacher allows peers to grade the work of each other or for parent volunteers to grade the work. The fear is that these practices would violate the *Family Educational Right and Privacy Act* (FERPA). In 2002, the U.S. Supreme Court heard the case of *Owasso Independent School District v. Falvo*, 534 U.S. 426 (2002). In a unanimous decision, the Court ruled in favor of the school district, and held that allowing students to score each other's tests, and even to call out the grades, does not violate the *Family Educational Rights and Privacy Act*. In the majority opinion, Justice Anthony Kennedy wrote, "Correcting a classmate's work can be as much a part of the assignment as taking the test itself. It is a way to teach material again in a new context, and it helps show students how to assist and respect fellow pupils."

Although I do not believe that calling out the grades publicly is a prudent practice, doing so is not a violation of FERPA. Peer grading, if handled in a way that protects the dignity of students, can be very beneficial in addition to be a time-saver for the teacher.

What Really Does Not Need to Be Done?

How many reports does your school generate simply because "that is the way we have always done it"? Doing well that which need not be done at all is a terrible waste of time. If you are trying to find time for worthwhile projects, getting rid of the unnecessary is a great place to start.

Maintaining Focus— Christmas Letter from the Future

Our culture is good at making New Years resolutions and poor at following through with them. We can see the big picture, but when the day-to-day activities of life get in the way, little progress is made towards the goals we set for ourselves.

For me, the "Christmas Letter from the Future" is a way that I remind myself of yearly goals. For many years, my wife and I have composed a Christmas letter and included it with the cards we mail each December. Like many couples, we have friends scattered across the country, and the Christmas letter serves as a way to keep others abreast of the major news in our lives.

In January 2006, I did something that seemed so small at the time, yet has produced remarkable dividends. On a January day, I composed the Christmas letter for the *coming* year just as I hoped it would actually read when December rolled around. Although it talks about events yet to come, it is written in the *past* tense, as if the subjects of which it speaks have already occurred. Every month, I do nothing more than reread that letter. The act serves as a monthly reminder of the direction we want our lives to take.

When December of that year arrived and it was time to write the real Christmas letter, the similarity between what had been written in January and what had materialized during the year was astonishing. Setting goals and keeping those goals in front of us is important. For me, this was the trick that caused me to do both. I have made writing the "Christmas Letter from the Future" an annual tradition, and offer it as a suggestion for helping you accomplish that which is important.

Next Steps

♦ Identify the time of day you want to establish as "quiet time."

♦ Plan how you will approach your "gatekeeper" and what instructions you will give.

♦ Decide what times of the day are best to check and handle voice-mail and e-mail.

- Identify the nonteaching tasks you perform that could be delegated to students. Structure a system for teaching the tasks and rotating the responsibilities.

- Examine ways that you can streamline the amount of time spent on grading papers and put the strategies into action.

- Examine your task list to determine what items need not be done at all and get rid of them.

- Consider adopting the practice of the "Christmas Letter from the Future." If it meets with your approval, add composing that letter to your repeating task list for each January.

Conclusion

Time is Your Friend

The master in the art of living makes little distinction between his work and his play, his labor and his leisure, his mind and his body, his information and his recreation, his love and his religion. He hardly knows which is which. He simply pursues his vision of excellence at whatever he does, leaving others to decide whether he is working or playing. To him he's always doing both.

— James Michener

This book began with a poem I stumbled upon quite a few years ago in a book entitled *The Harried Leisure Class* (1970). On the page facing that poem is a quote by Dennis Gabor, which reads simply, "Till now man has been up against nature; from now on he will be up against his own nature."

The demands of a changing world lead our society to do more, increase complexity, and ignore the finiteness of the time available. Our schools reflect these same tendencies, and teachers find themselves facing enormous demands with limited time in which to address them.

You hardly need anyone to point out these realities. More than likely, these are the very concerns that led you to this book. My hope is that this book has provided an understandable framework for managing that finite time. Our jobs are not the papers and e-mails that come at us from all sides. The inability to handle them, however, hampers our ability to be the best teachers we can be. Each chapter is crafted to give the reader the "nuts and bolts" of structuring a system equal to the demands of the job.

Every reader is different, and for this reason some strategies will resonate more than others with you. A colleague may read the same book and take from it entirely different ideas for organizing life and managing time. I hope that this book is one that will earn a place close at hand, complete with highlighted sentences, margins filled with notes, and pages dog-eared to mark their easy retrieval. Each reading is likely to reveal a nuance previously unrealized.

As this book comes to a close, I hope that you have found strategies to make your job easier, your stress level lower, and confidence in your ability to assume a strong leadership role at an all-time high. Teachers need the tools to make the complex simple, and this book aims to provide some of them.

Every good thing we do for our students, our school systems, our communities, our families, and ourselves is accomplished through the dimension of time. For the organized teacher, time is a friend.

Appendix A

Checklist for a Great Start

Off to a Great Start in a New School

As I wrote this book, I did so with three groups of teachers in mind: the teacher who is new to the profession, the teacher who is new to the school, and the teacher who simply wants to "turn over a new leaf" and *get organized*. Teachers in the first two groups face a tremendous learning curve. In addition to organizing a classroom and getting ready for the start of the school year, they must also learn their way around the building, learn where items are located, and get to know a variety of people in the school.

The following checklist provides a roadmap to help the teacher become acclimated to the new surroundings as quickly as possible. I imagine that during the first days and weeks on the job, these few pages will be referred to time and time again. The list is long, and its very length illustrates the challenge a teacher faces when he or she is new to the faculty.

♦ Have you met the following people at your school?

  ☐ Principal

  ☐ Assistant principal

  ☐ Guidance counselor

  ☐ School psychologist

  ☐ Special education team

- ☐ Teachers at your grade level
- ☐ Professional development coordinator
- ☐ Union representative
- ☐ Secretaries
- ☐ Nurse
- ☐ Custodians
- ☐ Cafeteria staff
- ☐ Librarian/media specialist
- ☐ Specialists that your class will see: PE, Art, Music, Foreign language
- ☐ Aides
- ☐ Mentor teacher
- ☐ President of the PTA or PTO
- ☐ School board members (if your principal thinks it's a good idea)

♦ Do you know where to find the following locations?
- ☐ Office
- ☐ Classrooms (Do you know where the other grade levels, wings, or pods are located?)
- ☐ Student bathrooms
- ☐ Staff bathrooms
- ☐ Library
- ☐ Media center
- ☐ Resource room/special education rooms
- ☐ Supply rooms
- ☐ Custodian's office/custodian's closet
- ☐ Cafeteria
- ☐ Auditorium
- ☐ Gymnasium/locker rooms
- ☐ Teachers' lounge

☐ Teachers' work room (copier, paper cutter, etc.)

☐ Playground area

☐ The door you should use for fire drills

☐ Where to stand during fire drills

◆ Do you have the following equipment available for use and do you know how to use?

☐ Copier

☐ Computers

☐ Projector

☐ TV/VCR or TV/DVD

☐ Slide projector

☐ Overhead projector

☐ Tape recorder

☐ Stereo

☐ Laminator

☐ Paper cutter

☐ Fax machine

☐ Die-cut machine

☐ Spiral book maker

☐ Laptops

☐ Overhead microscope

☐ Digital camera

◆ Do you know how to record the following information or find the following information?

☐ Attendance and tardies

☐ Lunch count

☐ Cumulative folders

☐ Report cards/progress reports

☐ Parent conference notes

☐ Phone conference records

☐ Professional development hours

☐ Sick day, professional day, funeral observance, etc. forms

☐ Expense reports

☐ Purchase orders

♦ Did you prepare the following items?

☐ Substitute folder

☐ Mailbox system for the students

☐ Portfolio system

☐ Curriculum folders

☐ Lesson plans

☐ Gradebook

♦ Do you know the following pieces of information?

☐ Legal responsibilities (IEPs and 504 plans)

☐ Norms of the school

☐ Transitions

☐ Going to assemblies

☐ Indoor recess

☐ Duties

☐ School discipline policy

☐ Procedures for sending kids out of the room for discipline

☐ Allowing kids to work in the room alone

☐ Allowing kids to go to the library or computer lab to work alone

☐ Policy for sending notes home

☐ Policy for when there are visitors to school (Do you send them to the office to sign in? Do they wear badges, etc.?)

☐ What to do with kids who arrive to school early

☐ What to do with kids who miss the bus home

☐ How to order supplies

- ☐ Procedures for using machines (Are there codes, specific times, aides who do the copying, etc.?)
- ☐ How to sign out AV equipment
- ☐ Procedures for rainy days
- ☐ Location of district offices
- ☐ Location of other district schools
- ☐ Location of public library
- ☐ Location of nearby museums
- ☐ Location of teacher supply stores
- ☐ How to get your paycheck or pay stubs
- ☐ Location of coffee and vending machines
- ☐ Procedures for line-up outside or in the gym
- ☐ School rules
- ☐ Recess rules
- ☐ Procedures for emergency drills
- ☐ Procedures for attending conferences or seminars
- ☐ Required paperwork for yourself
- ☐ Required paperwork to send home to families

♦ Do you know the following phone numbers and fax numbers (if applicable)?
- ☐ School
- ☐ Principal
- ☐ Mentor
- ☐ Grade level partners
- ☐ Substitute line
- ☐ Human Resources department
- ☐ District office
- ☐ Payroll department
- ☐ PTA/PTO President and Committee
- ☐ Other staff members

☐ Parents of all students

☐ Do you need a code to call out from your classroom or the school?

♦ Have you prepared the following things for getting your classroom ready?

☐ Bulletin boards

☐ Learning centers

☐ Classroom bookcases

☐ Name outside of door

☐ Class list outside of door

☐ Student name tags for desks, cubbies, locker area, or hooks

☐ Seating chart

☐ Schedule

♦ Have you gotten or do you know where to get the following supplies for you and the class?

☐ Plan book

☐ Gradebook

☐ Attendance sheets

☐ Lunch count sheets

☐ Copy paper

☐ Lined paper

☐ Graph paper

☐ Construction paper

☐ Notecards

☐ Staplers and staples

☐ Transparency paper and markers

☐ Chart paper

☐ Erasers

☐ Tape and dispensers

☐ Paper clips

- ☐ Chalk (colored and white) and erasers
- ☐ White board markers and erasers
- ☐ Pens
- ☐ Pencils
- ☐ Manila file folders
- ☐ Hanging folders and plastic tabs
- ☐ Pocket folders
- ☐ Rubber bands
- ☐ Scissors
- ☐ Rulers
- ☐ Glue and glue sticks
- ☐ Crayons
- ☐ Markers
- ☐ Blue books or composition books

♦ Do you have a plan for school-to-home communication?
- ☐ Emergency forms
- ☐ Classroom rules and policies for discipline, homework, and grading
- ☐ Volunteer forms
- ☐ E-mail forms
- ☐ Newsletters
- ☐ Class website
- ☐ Homework website
- ☐ Voicemail

♦ Do you have the materials you need to teach your lessons?
- ☐ Textbooks
- ☐ Teacher materials to go with textbooks
- ☐ Supplemental teaching materials (Other books, posters, videos, etc. to go with units)

☐ Library materials (Books and videos that are stored in your school library)

☐ Substitute folder

♦ Do you have these necessary materials?

☐ Keys to your room or the school

☐ Code to the machines

☐ Clock and PA system in your room

☐ Computer

☐ Enough file cabinets

☐ Enough student desks and chairs

☐ Teacher desk and chair

☐ Fan

☐ Class lists

☐ IEPs and 504 plans

☐ School calendar (know the dates of vacations, holidays, late starts or early releases, in-service days, special programs, annual school events, grading periods, report cards, progress reports, back-to-school night, parent conferences, meetings)

Special thanks to Jenny Cheifetz for providing this list. Because of the mobility of her family, she found herself "the new kid on the block" on a regular basis and having to adapt to new surroundings and new procedures. She writes, "I started to write a new teacher book but with small children, it never got finished." Ms. Cheifetz is now the owner of the Sugar Mommy, LLC in New Hampshire (www.TheSugarMommy.com). What she experienced by being the "new kid on the block" time and time again will now be of help to countless teachers as they begin both the excitement and challenge of accepting a new teaching position.

Appendix B

Configuring Outlook

Getting Acquainted with Outlook

When opening Outlook for the first time, you may receive a message asking if you want Outlook to be your default e-mail program. For now, answer "no" to that question. If you decide for sure that Outlook is the program for you, do not worry. Outlook will ask this question the next time and each time the program is opened until you finally answer "yes."

Outlook's prompts will guide the process of establishing an e-mail account. You will need to know what type of server is used to retrieve your e-mail (Microsoft Exchange Server, Pop3, IMP, HTTP, or other type of server). Secure this information from your service provider if you do not already know it. You will also need to know your e-mail address and password associated with your account.

These few steps will allow the most efficient use of Outlook:

1. On the left-hand side of the screen, notice the series of buttons similar to those shown in Figure B.1 (page 150). This area is called the *Navigation Pane*. Click the Calendar button.

Figure B.1. Selections in the Outlook Navigation Pane

2. From the menu bar at the top of the screen, choose View > Arrange By > Show Views in Navigation Pane. A series of radio buttons appear in the Navigation Pane.

3. Click the radio button that says Day/Week/Month (Figure B.2).

Figure B.2. Day-Week-Month View

4. We want to show the TaskPad if it is not already showing. From the menu bar, select View > TaskPad. In Outlook 2007, the TaskPad has been renamed To-Do Bar.

5. Select View > TaskPadView > Active Tasks for Selected Days (Outlook 2003 only).

6. Finally, return to View > TaskPad View. If Include Tasks With No Due Date does not have a check mark beside, click on that selection (Outlook 2003 only).

7. The finished product will resemble Figure B.3.

Figure B.3. Outlook Day-Week-Month View with TaskPad

The Outlook Calendar

Creating and working with appointments is very intuitive. To create a new appointment, simply click on the calendar and type the name for an appointment. Click the mouse somewhere else and Outlook accepts that appointment. For many of the appointments that you schedule, what we have just done is sufficient.

To change the start and end times of an appointment, click the line at the top or bottom of the appointment and drag it to another time. Click in the middle of the appointment, and the entire appointment can be dragged to another time slot.

Double-clicking on an appointment opens a dialog box and reveals a number of variables you can control (Figure B.4, page 152).

Figure B.4. New Appointment

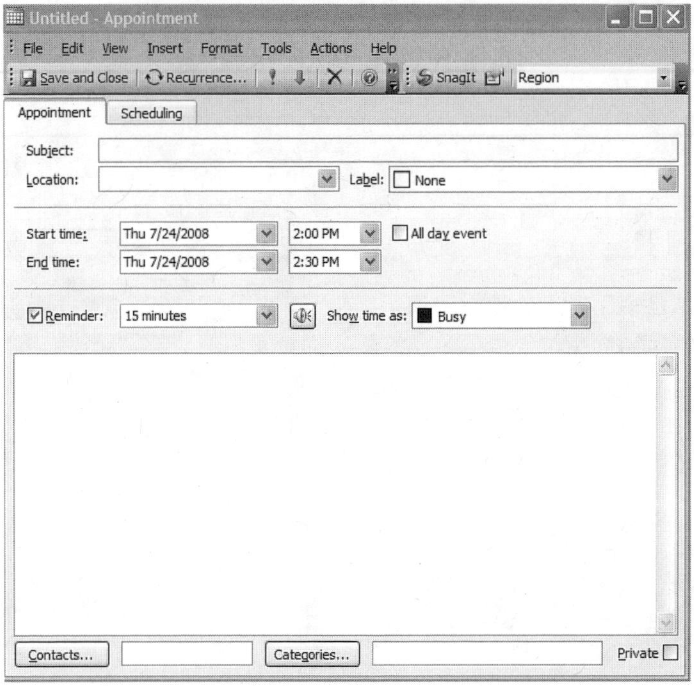

Using this dialog box, you can:

♦ Choose a starting and ending date for the appointment.

♦ Choose a starting and ending time.

♦ Click Recurrence for an appointment that will happen, for example, every Tuesday at 10:00 A.M.

♦ Set a reminder. A box will pop up and a chime will sound at the prescribed amount of time before the appointment.

♦ Enter notes related to the appointment. The large rectangular box provides a wealth of space to enter any details about that appointment.

All-Day Event

In addition to appointments (which happen on a particular day at a particular time), you will need to know how to create an all-day event. The difference between the two is that the all-day event is not tied to a particular time. to create an all-day event, right-click directly on the date at the top of the calendar. Choose New All-Day Event.

TaskPad (To-Do Bar)

Entering a new task could not be easier. When a new commitment presents itself, click where you see the message Click here to add a new Task and press Enter. The task now appears on the list. Tasks not completed today will simply be there tomorrow. Even better, the TaskPad takes the responsibility for doing your remembering.

The first step is to set up the TaskPad or To-Do Bar.

1. Right-click on the header just above the Click here to add a new Task message.

2. A menu appears. Select Customize Current View from that menu.

3. A dialogue box appears.

4. Click on Fields. You may now select the fields that will appear on the TaskPad or To-Do Bar.

5. Where you see Select available fields from, choose Frequently used fields.

6. On the left-hand side of the box, click on each of the following fields in order, and click Add between each one. The fields you will need are:

   ♦ Complete

   ♦ Subject

   ♦ Start Date

   ♦ Due Date

   ♦ Status (Select Status if using a BlackBerry; select Category if using a Palm)

   ♦ Notes

   ♦ Recurring

Figure B.5 (page 154) shows how the dialogue box will look. Before leaving this dialogue box, there is one more thing to do:

Figure B.5. Dialogue Box Showing Outlook Fields

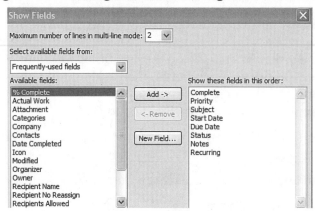

7. Click the Filter button.

8. Click the Advanced tab.

9. From the Field menu, select Frequently Used Fields > Complete.

10. The Condition box should be set to Equals.

11. Value should be No.

12. Click Add to List.

13. Click OK.

14. Click OK.

Figure B.6 shows the finished product.

Figure B.6. Outlook TaskPad Ready to Use

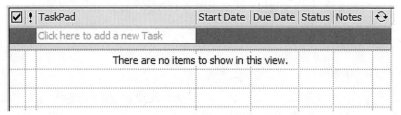

Entering Sample Tasks

At this point, try entering a few sample tasks. Click on the Click here to add a Task line, enter a sample task, and press Enter. The task will appear in the list. Experiment with setting a start date or due date by clicking in the appropriate column and choosing a date from the popup calendar. Notice that by pressing Tab, you move across from field to field.

Headers in the TaskPad or To-Do Bar

We can sort the list by clicking on any of the headers. Clicking on the Due Date header sorts the list so that tasks overdue appear at the top and tasks due far in the future are at the bottom. By clicking on the Status header, you will see all of the tasks Not Started together and all of the tasks where you are Waiting on Someone Else together. To add a secondary sort, hold the Shift key and click on a header.

Double-clicking a task displays the following elements over which the user has control. Figure B.7 shows the Task box.

Figure B.7. New Task

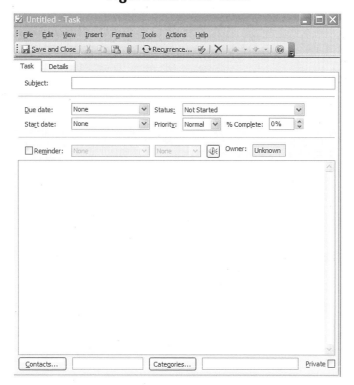

- ◆ The name of the task goes in the Subject line.

- ◆ A date can be set for the task to appear on the list and to come due.

- ◆ A repeating pattern for the task can be established, such a reminder to change the air filters at home the 1st day of every month or order laminating film for the school every July 10th.

- ◆ A large section allows for recording notes related to the task. If the task is a phone call, take notes in that section during the call.

If working on a project, list the first step in the subject line, and list the rest of known steps in the large note section.. When one step is complete, instead of checking it off as done, cut and paste the next one in the subject line. Chapter 6, "Handling Multiple Projects," discussed this concept in detail.

Keyboard Shortcuts

Outlook allows the user to perform common commands with keyboard shortcuts. The shortcuts are much quicker than using the mouse to select those commands from menus. The shortcuts worth memorizing are shown in Figure B.8.

Figure B.8. Keyboard Shortcuts

Keyboard Shortcut	Action Performed by Shortcut
Ctrl+Shift+A	Creates a new Appointment from anywhere in Outlook
Ctrl+Shift+C	Creates a new Contact from anywhere in Outlook
Ctrl+Shift+F	Creates an Advanced Find from anywhere in Outlook
Ctrl+Shift+K	Creates a new Task from anywhere in Outlook
Ctrl+Shift+M	Creates a new E-mail Message from anywhere in Outlook
Ctrl+Shift+N	Creates a new Note from anywhere in Outlook

Searching the Tasks

You can search your Tasks at any time. Click on the Task button on the left side of the screen. Enter the search term in the box at the top of the screen to

- Satisfy yourself that you had indeed put a particular Task on the list, even if the start date was not to occur for months.

- Find a particular item you know was added to the list but somehow do not see it.

- Find a piece of information imbedded in the note section of a Task.

- Find a piece of information either in the subject line or note section of a Task that completed sometime in the past.

Navigating the TaskPad or To-Do Bar

As you use the Outlook TaskPad, assigning a Start Date and Due Date will be a skill set used numerous times every day. Likewise, you will change the Start Date and Due Date on various tasks. Outlook offers shortcuts:

- ♦ You may select a Start Date and Due Date by clicking the arrow and navigating to a date using the calendar.

- ♦ You may type the date. For example, to enter the date "January 20, 2011," you could enter either "1/20/2011" or "1/20/11."

- ♦ If the date you wish to select is within the current month, simply enter the day of the month. For example, entering "20" and pressing Tab will enter the 20th day of the current month.

- ♦ If the date you wish to enter is within the next 12 months, you may enter the month and day. For example, entering "1/20" and pressing Tab will assign a date for the next January 20th.

In Chapter 3, we learned about organizing the list according to Due Date. We could then move tasks up or down the list by simply manipulating the Due Date. You will find when entering a Due Date and pressing Enter, the cursor moves down to the Due Date field of the task below it. You can quickly alter the Due Date on a number of tasks by simply going down the list entering the day of the month and pressing Enter.

Maintaining Your Data

Backup Your pst File

Your Outlook data is valuable, and you certainly do not want to lose it because of a hard drive failure or problems with corruption. A critical concept to understand is that all of your Outlook data is located in *one file*. The extension of that file is pst. More than likely, the name of the file will be Outlook.pst.

To backup your Outlook data, you need to know the location of that pst file. To find it, go to File > Data File Management. Click on the line that begins Personal Folders and then click the Settings button. In the box that appears, look at the Filename line for the location of your Outlook data. Figure B.9 (page 158) illustrates what you will see.

Figure B.9. Location of pst File

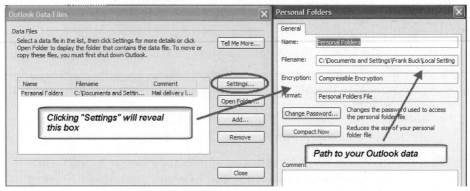

Close Outlook before attempting to copy the Outlook.pst file; otherwise, Outlook will return an error message. Likewise, any other program that communicates with your Outlook.pst file should be closed. For example, if you synchronize Outlook to a handheld device, the program that manages your synchronization should be closed.

Now, simply navigate to the Outlook.pst file. Right-click on it and choose Copy. Open My Documents and choose Paste. You now have a copy of your data in My Documents. The next time you make a backup of My Documents, a copy of your Outlook data will be included in this backup. Even better yet, paste that pst file into your Current Projects folder. The next time you backup Current Projects, you will also be making a backup of the your Outlook data. Outlook Personal Folders Backup is a free tool that simplifies the process. This tool is available from Microsoft.

Scanpst.exe

Scanpst.exe is a handy tool for diagnosing and repairing errors in the pst file. Locating it can be tricky. I have found the easiest solution is to simply do a search for scanpst. Once the search locates the file, right-click on it and create a shortcut. Drag the shortcut into your Fingertip file. You run this tool by double-clicking on it and following the simple instructions. Close Outlook and any other program that may be accessing your Outlook data before running the program; otherwise, an error message will display. Running scanpst.exe once a month serves as excellent preventive maintenance.

AutoArchive

AutoArchive removes older items from your pst file and stores them in an archive file. The best course for the new Outlook user is to simply turn off this feature. To perform this function, go to Tools > Options. Click the Other

Tab and then the AutoArchive button. Uncheck the box which says Run Auto-Archive every ___ days. Figure B.10 shows how your screen will appear.

Figure B.10. AutoArchive Settings

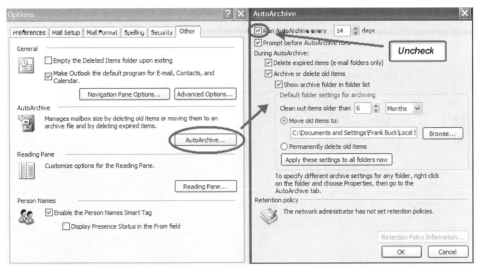

Once you have become experienced with Outlook, you should use Auto-Archive. Simply return to the same screen shown in Figure B.10 and click the box to turn AutoArchive on. You will select how often AutoArchive will run and how old items must be before they are archived. The critical element here is that you do not allow your Notes to be autoarchived. To prevent the Notes from being autoarchived do the following (Figure B.11, page 160):

1. Select Go > Folder List.

2. Right-click on the Notes icon.

3. Select Properties.

4. Click the AutoArchive tab.

5. Click the Do not archive items in this folder radio button.

6. Click Apply and OK.

Figure B.11. Preventing Autoarchiving of Notes

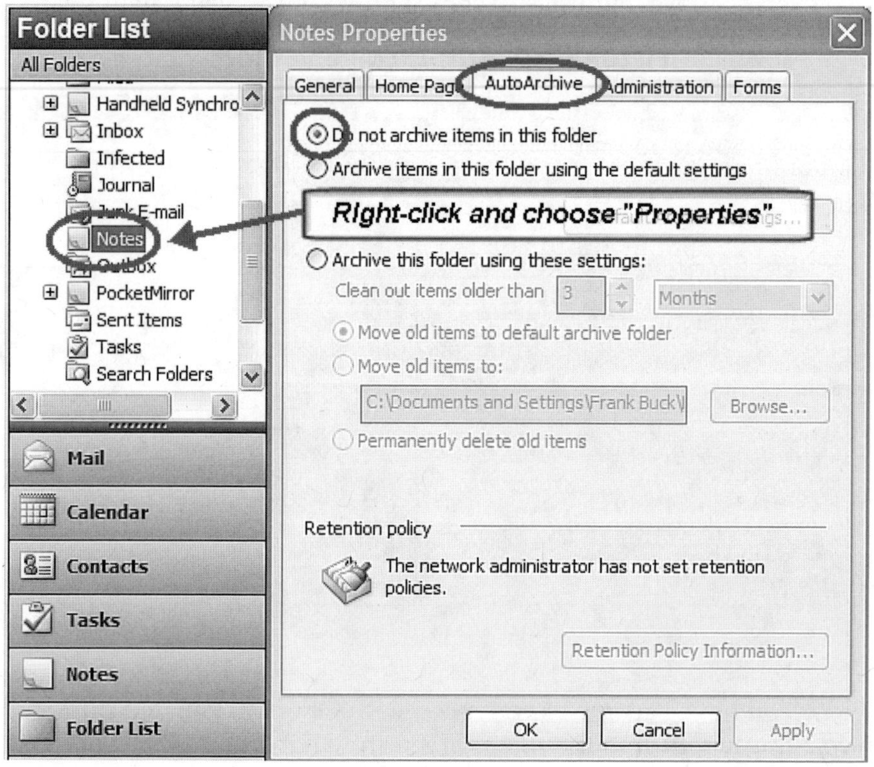

Conclusion

Please refer back to this Appendix for the technical aspects involved with Outlook. The instructions here will allow you to get full benefit of the strategies in Chapter 3. As this book goes to press, both Outlook 2003 and Outlook 2007 are widely in use. The similarity in the two versions allows the strategies for use to be the same and the illustrations to be usable both those using either version. The coming years are sure to produce additional upgrades and a host of programs yet to be conceived.

The principles we examined in this book, however, are timeless. Teachers, both now and in the future, will function in a complex world and require tools that make the complex simple. An understanding of the methodology in this book allows you to fashion any number of tools, both paper-based and digital-based, into tools to help organize your life and manage your time.

References

Buck, F. (2008) *Get Organized!: Time Management for School Leaders*. New York: Eye On Education.

Clark, R. (2003). *The Essential 55*. New York: Hyperion.

Drucker, P. F. (1966). *The effective executive*. New York: Harper & Row.

Hobbs, C. R. (1987). *Time power*. New York: Harper & Row.

Linder, S. B. (1970). *The harried leisure class*. New York: Columbia University Press.

Mackenzie, R. A. (1972). *The time trap: How to get more done in less time*. New York: McGraw-Hill.

Mackenzie, A. (1990). *The time trap*. New York: AMACOM.

Peterson, W. A. (1968). *Adventures in the art of living*. New York: Simon and Schuster.